The Search Committee
HANDBOOK

Sponsored by
American Association for Higher Education

in partnership with
Academic Search Consultation Service

with support from
The Atlantic Philanthropies (USA), Inc.

The Search Committee
HANDBOOK

A Guide to Recruiting Administrators

Second Edition, Revised

THEODORE J. MARCHESE
and
JANE FIORI LAWRENCE
Assisted by CAITLIN ANDERSON

STERLING, VIRGINIA

Published by Stylus Publishing, LLC
22883 Quicksilver Drive
Sterling, Virginia 20166-2102

Book design and composition by Susan Mark
Coghill Composition Company
Richmond, Virginia

Library of Congress Cataloging-in-Publication-Data

Marchese, Theodore J.
    The search committee handbook : a guide to recruiting administrators / Theodore J.
Marchese and Jane Fiori Lawrence ; assisted by Caitlin Anderson.—2nd ed., rev.
        p.   cm.
    Includes index.
    ISBN 1-57922-177-7 (pbk. : alk. paper)
    1. College administrators—United States—Recruiting—Handbooks, manuals, etc.
    I. Lawrence, Jane Fiori.   II. Anderson, Caitlin.   III. Title.

    LB2331.6952.M37   2005
    371.1'11—dc22

                                                            2005051642

ISBN: 1-57922-177-7 (paper) / 13-digit ISBN: 978-1-57922-177-5

Printed in Canada

All first editions printed on acid free paper that meets the
American National Standards Institute Z39-48 Standard.

Bulk Purchases
Quantity discounts are available for
use in workshops and staff development.
Call 1-800-232-0223

First edition published by AAHE, 1987
Second edition published by AAHE, 2005
Second edition, revised, published by Stylus Publishing, 2006

10 9 8 7 6 5 4 3 2 1

Contents

Boxes

Introduction

In 1987, when the American Association for Higher Education (AAHE) published the first edition of our *Search Committee Handbook*, we expected it to remain useful over a period of many years. Its messages seemed timeless and commonsensical: think deeply about the position you'll fill, recruit widely, treat candidates with respect, do your homework on them, help your appointee succeed. Indeed, three printings and 30,000 copies later, all those messages pertain today.

But over time the contexts for search and the ways it might be done have changed. Many advances have come from technology. Fax machines, the Internet and Web, audio- and videoconferencing, for example, enable things like the paperless search, travel-free interviewing, and desktop research about candidates and institutions. Today, virtually all administrative openings are posted on the *Chronicle of Higher Education*'s website; it receives tens of thousands of hits a week. The "HR" function on many campuses is now more developed. Federal and state regulations about hiring and employment have grown apace. The use of search firms has expanded from the presidency to searches for vice presidents, deans, and other administrative posts. Our student bodies have changed, too, increasing the need for faculty-staff diversity even as the legal boundaries for achieving it narrow.

The most significant—and least understood—change is the recent sharp decline in the size of applicant pools for administrative posts. In 1987, search committees placed ads and watched confidently as 100 to 200 applications arrived in the mail. Today, the same ads might bring 20 to 40 applications. A recent dean's search at an Ohio university attracted five applicants, two of them from inside.

The reasons for this sharp drop in the size of pools are many, albeit speculative. The tragic events of September 11, 2001, may have played a role in convincing more professionals to adopt a "stay put" mentality toward their homes and careers. The cumulative effects of poor treatment in prior searches deter candidates from entering subsequent searches. The phenomena of dual careers, promotion from within, housing market distortions, restrictive pension rules, and geographic preference also keep candidates from moving. Too, able young faculty and staff look at the work demands that come with an administrative position, and at the revolving doors through which middle and senior managers come and go, and decide to pass on the "opportunity."

———◆———

All these factors add up to a different—and more challenging—set of tasks for campus leadership and search committees. Given these changes, we became convinced that a new version of *The Search Committee Handbook* was needed. Happily that view was shared by The Atlantic Philanthropies (USA) Inc., which provided a grant to AAHE in partnership with the Academic Search Consultation Service to support the work behind this new version. As with the first edition (supported by the Exxon Educational Foundation and TIAA-CREF), we were able to put together a national advisory board of experienced scholars and practitioners; undertake extensive literature reviews; conduct six focus groups around the country on topics of search; speak with committee chairs about their experiences;

do autopsies on failed searches; and engage search veterans to review successive drafts. At the end of this *Handbook* we acknowledge the many people who helped us most, though all errors of judgment and reporting belong to the authors.

Because the world of search will see further changes over time and because of continuing need for advice on hiring, our Atlantic Philanthropies project included funding to establish a website with additional and updated resources for search. Visit www.thesearchsource.org at the start of any search, and use it to provide feedback on this *Handbook*. Campuses doing presidential or faculty searches also will value the articles, forms, and links to websites they'll find there.

This *Handbook* focuses on administrative searches below the level of the presidency—the searches for vice presidents, deans, directors, and coordinators for which appointment of a search committee is the norm. We exclude presidential searches because these necessarily involve trustees or regents and parties beyond campus, and because they are almost universally served by consultants. We exclude faculty searches because they involve processes and norms that are discipline- or field-specific. Even so, the basics of good practice in hiring are not position-dependent or unique to higher education; anyone with responsibilities to search and hire will find points to ponder in these pages.

As before, this *Handbook* was written for practitioners—for the institutional leaders who will plan the search, form the committee, and later make the appointment, and for the chair and members of the search committee itself. The first two chapters and the final one are addressed primarily to the senior appointing officer; all that lies between (chapters 3 through 6) is written with the committee most in mind.

We are aware that colleagues from abroad may find this *Handbook* on the Web and (we suspect) be puzzled by it. As much as the authors admire and learn from universities abroad, we made an explicit choice to limit our discussion here to a U.S. higher education context. The ways that a university recruits professional talent tell a lot, of course, about underlying values. The values you see in here are those ascendant in the recent life of

U.S. universities—a participative process, open to a wide range of talent, in search of an administration that will serve and lead.

The sheer breadth of American higher education is a marvel: we celebrate our vigorous community colleges, national research universities, fine liberal arts colleges, seminaries, technical schools, women's colleges, HBCUs, and so on. Beyond these types, there are differences of public and private, religious and secular, union and nonunion, sunshine law or not; within types, each institution enjoys its own history, culture, and clientele. Writing a single handbook to cover all these differences falls somewhere between daunting and foolhardy. What we've tried to do, with the help of talented reviewers from different sectors, is capture a sense of best practice across the widest spectrum of institutions and cultures. Users of this *Handbook* should be alert to this fact and assertive in adapting our advice to their own situation and culture.

Also note that this *Handbook* is organized around the usual, successive steps in an "ideal" search: first you figure out what you are looking for (chapters 1 and 2), then recruitment proceeds (chapter 4), followed by the screening (chapter 5), and on through an appointment (chapter 7). In reality, the life of a search committee is not always so rational or ideal . . . "stuff happens," so committees find themselves backtracking, skipping ahead, or coming to a halt. Further, people are busy, time presses, resources are pinched, politics intrude, and no committee can pursue every good idea.

Read this *Handbook*, then, not like a cookbook, full of required and sequenced steps, but like a guidebook, pointing you toward destinations, events, and paths to pursue. You know best your own campus and what is possible within your situation; use this *Handbook* as a fund of ideas from which better, more thoughtful practice will ensue.

Best of luck with your search!

Theodore J. Marchese
Jane F. Lawrence
Washington, D.C., and Merced, California
October 4, 2004

The Search Committee HANDBOOK

CHAPTER 1

The Vacancy:
An Organizational Opportunity

Campus leaders know that nothing they do is more important than to recruit, nurture, and advance the talents of line managers and administrative staff, who make their college or university work. When an administrative vacancy occurs, they see it as a dual opportunity for their institution: first to rethink a function—the role and goals of a position, and the character of person needed to make it work—then to make an appointment that helps to achieve them.

To get it right—to initiate a search process with high probability of an effective appointment—campus leaders start not with a search committee but with a process of thought. They rethink the position in question, knowing that "position analysis" is essential to a committee's subsequent search and an appointment that meets an institution's goals.

Position analysis precedes a search because so much is at stake in top-level administrative appointments. The right person set on the right course brings benefits for years, while an ill-founded appointment can bring real harm. Campus leaders know that when a person doesn't work out or an office underperforms, the deeper reasons are often organizational and not a function of the person. Leaders want to know those reasons, and address them now, so that the subsequent search and appointment have a best shot at success.

This first chapter, then, starts with how to rethink a vacant position. It begins with steps of position analysis, driven by the five questions that follow. After those questions and advice on how they might be addressed, we think more broadly about your institution as an employer and the consequent likelihood that it will be able to attract the talent it needs. We end with short sections

on the appropriate use of committees for search and on promotion from within.

Questions for an Appointing Officer

What questions should drive a position analysis?

A first question, too seldom asked, is, **What would happen if this job were not filled or performed?** Is it possible to transfer essential functions of the job to other offices? To subcontract them? Or to promote someone to the job and reallocate part of that person's previous responsibilities?

At higher administrative levels, the answer to these questions will often be "no." Even so, it is always important for institutional officers to step back and ask, "Can these tasks be achieved in new ways?"

For midlevel posts, a political reality is that no organizational unit will ever volunteer to give up a position or budget line. Senior officers might challenge the unit with the vacancy by raising the question, "If all present resources were retained, what better uses for them could you devise than filling this slot?"

Question two is related: **Are there ways to realign this position to enhance institutional effectiveness** and attract higher-quality candidates? An open position presents opportunities to address structural inefficiencies or dysfunctions in existing operations. For example, if university communications has always reported to the chancellor's office, might gains be realized by integrating it instead into the university's information services operation? Might the college's office of planning and institutional research serve better by reporting to the provost instead of the president (or vice versa)? Instead of reporting to the vice president for finance, what benefits could accrue if facilities management reported to the campus planning office? Again, the objectives are institutional effectiveness and the success of the new appointment. Politically, it is often only when there is a vacancy—when personalities and turf behaviors are less in play—that these kinds of questions can be asked.

Question three: **Given the institution's mission and strategic goals, what background and abilities might the college or university need in the position, to meet its own agendas?**

An institution under state mandate to do something in the name of assessment, for example, may want to fill an institutional research vacancy with a person who understands the analysis of student learning outcomes. A college or university planning a capital campaign may look for a chief development officer with strengths in campaign management. A university under mandate to partner with schools in a K–16 initiative may well look for a new dean for its School of Education who accepts and will advance that agenda. In each case, leaders are asking, "Does the institution itself have needs that should drive this appointment?"

This is decidedly the moment, too, to pull out the strategic plan. So often in recruitment there is a big disconnect between the larger thrust or agendas of an institution and its conduct of particular searches. If your institution wants to become more entrepreneurial or customer oriented, teach at a distance or emphasize sponsored research, focus on better legislative relations, or build a faculty and staff that looks more like its student body, now is the moment to put those values front and center in your thinking about the position and the coming search.

Question four is related to the previous one: **What larger developments in society, higher education, or within the position's field might prompt different ways of thinking about the position?**

A good example from the 1990s was offered by the convergence of computing and telecommunications, which prompted many institutions to seek out a high-level "czar" to sort out and direct its costly information-technology investments. Similarly, fast-moving developments in information sciences have changed what many schools look for in a "head librarian." Job titles like "registrar" and "director of public relations" and "dean of extension" continue even as there have been significant evolutions in the role and expectations for the position.

Question five: **What can we learn from our past experience with this position?** Has it been a continual trouble area? What are the sources of its problems? Has it been marked by high turnover? Why? What accounts for the present vacancy? What does any of this tell us about (a) the position (does it need redefinition?) and (b) what we should look for in an appointment?

These are the questions that a vacancy provides occasion to answer. They are not the "who" questions of the search committee but the "what" questions for the leadership of the institution: What do we need from this position? What agenda do we advance with its filling?

Leadership's failure to answer them at the start, more than a missed opportunity, verges on the irresponsible. At the least, it can set in motion a search doomed to disappointment.

Arriving at Answers

Responsibility for analyzing the newly vacant position rests primarily with the officer to whom the office reports—a provost, for example, rethinks a vacant deanship, or a student affairs vice president an opening for a director of residence life. A good rule is that at least one person higher in the line of authority should become involved, if nothing else as a guard against token or too-narrow review. For positions of campuswide importance, the president and cabinet will want to take an active interest, along with the appointing officer, in defining broad directions for the position.

For major vacancies that raise wider questions of institutional direction—a vacant vice presidency, for example, or a director of athletics—the chief executive and cabinet should devote time to asking the questions posed above before any aspect of "search" seems to begin. (But note: this *is* the start of search.) They may consult national reports and their authors, invite opinion from within the faculty and staff, confer with key parties within the unit of vacancy, do likewise with people in the state served by the unit, read annual reports and self-studies, and order up analyses from the office of institutional research. Following all this, they might convene a brief retreat to sort options and set an agenda.

Not every vacancy, of course, will be so problematic or issue-laden that it requires so full a dose of introspection and planning. The significance of the appointment and what issues it may raise will govern the involvement by senior officers. Short of a full-blown review, which is necessary on most campuses for at least one position a year, here are three alternatives:

1. The appointing officer might accomplish the staff work on the vacancy and present a succinct, two-page plan for the position and its future to the president's cabinet. The role of senior management becomes that of oversight, of raising questions and providing suggestions, after which responsibility for proceeding returns to the appointing officer.

2. At a higher level of administrative involvement, the president might designate a small team of senior officers to work with the appointing officer to define broad directions for the position and its filling.

3. A consultant might be engaged at this early point to help with the position analysis; a team of two or three might be brought in for an especially complex appointment (e.g., an IT director). Consultants can shorten time-lines, ask pointed "outsider" questions, and provide expert, more objective advice.

If a professional search firm has been engaged it will expect to participate in your work of position analysis. Some firms with a management-consulting perspective refuse search assignments for which they haven't first had a chance to do this up-front work. "Unless I can be sure the institution knows precisely and accurately what I should be searching for," one consultant told us, "it's wasting my time and their money."

Over the years, we've heard story after story of failed searches. More often than not, the search entailed a committee hastily assembled, poorly charged and supported, which at last brought forward nominees only to have them brushed aside as "not what we're looking for." The missing ingredient in failed searches so often turns out to be that nobody took the time to do the necessary analysis and communicate beforehand "what we're looking for." The situation begs for outrage over the many hours of lost professional time and the lost appointment.

A search committee is an instrument for identifying talent. But it is the *institution's leaders*, not the committee, who make the appointment and live with the consequences. And so—one last time—campus leaders must think through and convey beforehand what the position requires.

Your Institution as Employer

Many factors crucial to the outcome of a search are beyond the control of a search committee; they have to do with institutional characteristics (such as your location) and with the position itself (e.g., what the salary is). Some of these matters an officer or committee cannot do much about: for example, whether you are public or private, rural or urban, two-year or four-year. But other factors are within the reach of institutional managers;

USING A SEARCH CONSULTANT

Jean Dowdall

Search consultants are widely used in higher education. What do they do? Does your search need a consultant? If so, how can you select the right one?

Search consultants assist institutions with the process of filling critical positions.

♦ **Consultants work for the institution, not for the individual candidate.** Consultants are paid by and serve the institution, not any particular candidate. Ultimately, the institution selects the person to be appointed, and the consultant's job is to support the selection process.

♦ **Consultants actively recruit candidates.** After working with campus representatives to analyze institutional needs, the consultant targets people in positions that provide preparation for the kind of position that is being filled (e.g., in a provost search, the consultant might target associate provosts and deans), focusing on similar institutions or institutions that have faced similar challenges, evaluating those people and encouraging strong prospects to become candidates. If the committee wants to consider candidates from outside higher education, the consultant uses networks in those areas to identify prospects. The consultant should bring familiarity with the candidates; knowledge of candidates' strengths and weaknesses helps the committee to focus quickly on the best prospects.

♦ **Consultants check candidate references and background** with particular skill. Consultants generally phone references rather than requesting letters of reference. They should be skilled interviewers, able to listen between the lines and draw out subtle concerns. Many consultants know the people they are calling for references, increasing the likelihood that the reference will be frank. Most consultants also check databases that gather press reports and other public information about candidates.

♦ **Consultants support the entire search process.** Although each consultant works somewhat differently, there are several things that most consultants do in addition to recruiting and evaluating candidates. For example, they help to clarify institutional issues and position expectations at the start of the search, they address difficult issues that arise during the search process, and they support the committee chair in tasks like setting the search schedule and managing candidate contacts.

The use of consultants has become widespread in searches for senior administrators (presidents, vice presidents, etc.). But consultants are rarely used in searches for lower-level positions (associate vice presidents, directors). One important reason for using a consultant is the risk associated with making a mistake. If a presidential or vice presidential search concludes without an appointment being made, this can be disruptive—it is a rather public failure that raises questions about why the institution couldn't attract and appoint a strong candidate, and it may slow progress on important activities like fund-raising or strategic planning. A consultant provides reassuringly broad experience in the search process, familiarity with candidates, and thus a kind of insurance policy that the search will come to a successful and timely conclusion.

Another reason why searches for senior positions are more likely to be assisted by consultants is cost. Typically consultant fees are about one-third of the salary that the position will be paying, plus expenses. Many institutions view this as too large an investment to make in a lower-level search.

Consultants can be helpful, but there are also reasons why an institution might not use a consultant.

♦ **Some institutions believe they don't need consultants.** Typically these are institutions that are so well known, or have such an attractive location, that they feel they can attract candidates on their own, just by advertising the position and perhaps contacting a few colleagues for suggestions.
♦ **Some institutions have a tradition of not using consultants**; they have successfully done searches on their own and see no reason to change.
♦ **Many institutions are concerned about the cost.**
♦ **Some critics will say that a consultant just brings in the same old predictable candidates**, with no excitement or spark of creativity in the candidate pool; can't search committee members find the latter on their own? The answer to that question is, yes, you can do much of this work on your own. But it takes time to do the work, knowledge of what needs to be done, and a network of relationships in higher education to call on.

If you want to consider using a consultant, how should you select the best firm for your search? Some firms or individual consultants specialize in certain kinds of positions, such as student-affairs professionals or chief information officers. Others focus on working with certain types of institutions (e.g., research universities or church-related colleges).

With all these choices, how can you find a search consultant? Check with the relevant professional association (e.g., National Association of College and University Business Officers for finance and administration positions). Look at ads in publications like the *Chronicle of Higher Education* and see which consultants are working with institutions and in positions like yours. And ask colleagues at other institutions who have recently worked with consultants about their experience.

To select the right consultant for your search, gather essential information before making your choice:

♦ Request and review proposals from the firms that seem suitable.
♦ Interview the consultants by phone or in person. Make sure you speak to the individual consultant who would handle your search; this person will work closely with you and will represent you to your candidates, so you want to be comfortable with this person.
♦ Ask references what it is really like to work with this consultant.

Just like your search for the best candidate for the position you are filling, a careful search for a search consultant is a good investment.

Dr. Dowdall is vice president of the search firm Witt/Kieffer.

attention to them now will be important to the success of any forthcoming search.

A good entry point for getting at the "manageables" is to ask, What do candidates look for in a position? Most want a sense of advancement, plus a competitive salary and benefits; these are givens. But most, too, want more than this: an institution they can be proud to work for, a sense of contribution, if not mission, in their work, good colleagues, and a fair chance to be successful. How does the position you'll soon advertise stack up along these lines? Your answers have everything to do with getting talented people to say yes to your recruitment and yes to a job offer.

An instructive example—when Northeastern University wound up recently on a list of "100 Best Places to Work" in the Boston area, all of its searches suddenly had greater numbers of talented people in them. Of course, there was nothing "sudden" at all about that development. It reflected years of intentional work to make that university, long overshadowed, into an employer of choice.

———◆———

Before a search commences, the appointing officer has to think carefully about the salary of the position. You don't want to overpay, of course, or throw institutional scales out of whack, but you know there is a competitive market for administrative talent and that what you're prepared to offer will have a significant impact on recruitment and acceptance. It's not that hard to do the homework here. CUPA-HR, the College and University Professional Association for Human Resources, publishes annual surveys of administrative salaries. Many institutions also have access to comparative salary information within their state system, consortium, or a data-sharing service.

Let it be noted, however, that more than a few searches these days come up empty because the offered salary was just too low. Institutional leaders should recognize that what happened earlier on the faculty side—market-driven differential pay by field—has now happened on the administrative side. Until recently, an administrator's place on an organization chart more or less predicted his or her pay. Now, especially in

crucial, high-demand fields where the talent is scarce and avidly competed for, salaries have jumped. Chief enrollment, development, and IT officers come to mind here. Now is the time, then, to ponder this fact: a search has to offer a competitive salary to attract a competitive pool.

In the past, institutions tended to be diffident about the salary associated with a position ("salary commensurate with experience"), often to everyone's dismay at the time of an offered appointment. Today, best practice entails being up-front with potential candidates about salary and benefits. If a certain salary won't work, the candidate and institution should know that at the start.

The other part of the equation is benefits, which ad writers in the *Chronicle of Higher Education* always claim will be "competitive." But those benefits, when looked at more closely, often turn out to be pretty spotty, with cobbled rules about retirement contribution, diminished support for health insurance, and little recognition or support for family situations or professional development. Further, many campuses do a poor job of describing benefit packages, sending potential applicants a mish-mash of pamphlets written for other purposes. Candidates absolutely notice these things; now, before recruitment begins, is the time for an institution to address the content and description of benefits.

———◆———

Candidates also, for reasons of career and sanity, want a job in which they can succeed. No one wants to fail; smart candidates look closely at the history of a position and at what happened to their predecessors, at the interpersonal atmosphere of the office, the reasonableness of demands placed upon it, the resources available, and so on. Patterns of low morale and high turnover, of administrative infighting, faculty–administration distrust, contentious unionism, a struggling presidency, board-level wrangling, and state or denominational intrusion will be noticed. Indeed, they may be the downfall of a search.

———◆———

If an office or department is dysfunctional, don't expect a search to solve that problem. If personnel changes need to be made for an office to function properly, make them now. One of the worst things an institution can do is to dump past mistakes and leftover issues on a new appointee who arrives with scant knowledge of the culture and little or no political base. The point of a search is not to pick someone and wish him or her luck, but to create conditions for a professional's success, which then becomes the institution's success.

Again, institutional factors and climate will have everything to do with your success in attracting talent. The blame for failed searches falls often on search committees when the real barriers were organizational. Many times a college would be better off appointing an interim or talented troubleshooter to straighten things out before commencing a search.

If the work of position redefinition described in this chapter has led to some form of restructuring or change in the scope and role of the position, now—before the search starts—is the time to announce and explain that change. Again, an institution shouldn't burden the newcomer with explaining to new colleagues changes that he or she had no part in making.

Search by Committee?

A next point—one that your institution may already have clear policies about—is whether this vacancy requires a search committee. If there is no policy, or the situation seems ambiguous, here are thoughts on use of the device.

Administrative search committees became the norm in academe only in recent decades. Like the public posting of vacancies that came in with them, the committee as an instrumentality of search came about as the result of struggles to democratize and make the governance of institutions more participative. They succeeded earlier years of appointment making done in contexts of paternalistic governance and reliance on old-boy networks.

On paper, the use of broadly representative committees for search represents progress. They reflect the more open, participatory ethos of today's higher education and legitimize an appointment as no other method can. They reflect, too, a commonsense notion that in judging talent, several heads can be better than one. By bringing a wide spectrum of minds (faculty minds especially) to bear on administrative appointments, wiser, more broadly acceptable choices become possible.

A good committee, as we'll see, becomes a bridge across campus constituencies, a consultant to institutional officers, and a champion for a new appointee. Undoubtedly, search committees have been a factor in breaking the hold of closed networks and opening doors for the advancement of women and minorities within administrative ranks. And, not least, for the people who serve on them, these committees provide an opportunity for service, create bonds of trust across campus silos, and offer an education in institutional realities.

The deficiencies of a committee-led process must also be acknowledged. The use of the search committee raises to a new order the amount of precious professional time invested in search. A committee, other things being equal, will always take longer to accomplish the same tasks. In judging talent, a committee is open to the charge that its internal needs for agreement "level down" searches, that committee action seldom results in the unusual but brilliant appointment. And, for all the positive outcomes that might be realized through committee service, a poorly conceived search process can frustrate its members and divide a campus community.

Taken together, the arguments convince us that in most situations a committee is very much worth it, if not essential. Several of the benefits of a committee-driven process are otherwise unobtainable, while most of its "cons" are avoidable. Still, none of the benefits comes with a guarantee, and there are pitfalls galore. Our aim in this *Handbook* is to spur your thinking and increase the odds for a positive outcome.

———◆———

A preference for use of search committees should not mean, however, a mindless application of the device to every vacancy no matter what. We came across one institution, for example, so enamored of participatory process that virtually any vacancy resulted in a campuswide search committee, including one for a purchasing agent in the business office. The tremendous cost in time and human resources raised by the search committee process alone should signal its selective use.

Based upon discussions with faculty and staff from a wide spectrum of institutions, a good rule emerges: the full search-committee process should be evoked only for positions of school or campuswide significance, for line positions and not staff, and for which there exist a variety of constituent interests that require voice in the filling of the position.

Under this rule, almost any vice presidency or deanship would require a search committee; so would a division chair (because of the interest of divisional faculty in the appointment); as would a director of admissions or registrar. But a search for an assistant to the president or an assistant dean, in the absence of line responsibilities, would not be committee driven. (The "constituents" of these positions, and their focus of accountability, are chiefly the president and dean, not the institution at large.)

Alternatives to a Full Search

The advantages of the search-committee process are marked enough that many institutions use trimmed-down versions of it for within-unit vacancies. For a counselor position in the student-health center, for example, one hardly needs to invoke a campuswide committee, presidential introspection, or elaborate interviews. At a Midwest university, we observed a team of three student-affairs professionals carry off just such a trimmed-down search with dispatch. At a Tennessee community college, a dean and two faculty members formed a "work group" to find a new director of a media resources center. Within the library at an Eastern urban university, "interviewing panels" help at the final stages of search for key staff positions. Most institutions, too, in hiring academic affairs staff, find ways to elicit faculty advice prior to an appointment.

A full search-committee process can take three to five months (or longer) to unfold. What should be done when the calendar doesn't allow such time, when a vacancy arises in June that must be filled by August? The universal advice is, appoint an acting or interim head of the office and commence a search the next fall; rushing things can lead to mistakes.

———◆———

What if the vacancy arises in, say, April; there is no person who can be appointed an "acting"; and the position *must* be filled soon? In these conditions, when the time for search and appointment is critically short, institutions have tried shortcut modifications of the process. Here are two we've seen:

- The appointing officer, upon completion of the position analysis, names a small committee to oversee the work of the search, recruits a pool, chooses the finalists, and uses the committee only for intensive interviewing and reference checking at the end (an "advise and consent" model).
- Another "emergency" process entails the appointing officer and committee combining roles to do the position analysis and post the vacancy. They then get out on the networks to locate individual candidates, talk to good ones as soon as they emerge, and then hire the first who looks capable of the job and is willing to take it (the "shoot with a rifle, not a shotgun" model).

Both of these procedures are risky. They cut corners and raise chances for a costly mistake. They lose for you many of the potential benefits of the fuller process and can endanger the legitimacy of an appointment. And they can be used to frustrate affirmative action goals (to realize them, too). They may in fact be flatly forbidden by applicable regulations, state law, a collective-bargaining agreement, or by institutional policy.

Experienced hands at search conclude what's been said in this section with a maxim: Improvisation invites disappointment. Every institution should be clear in advance (in writing) about which vacancies will invoke a search-committee process, and about what variances become permissible in stated circumstances.

Promotion from Within

There is a final matter for thought raised by a vacancy that institutional leaders can profitably ponder at this point. It comes from the fact that recruitment of talent from outside the institution can be costly in time and money, risky as to the result, and damaging to morale.

In many best-run corporations and professional firms, external recruitment is done only under extraordinary circumstances. Their rule is to hire carefully at the entry level, nurture the people you have, monitor performance and alter the job if necessary, do succession planning, then promote from within.

In too many colleges, by contrast, the rule seems to be "Use 'em and lose 'em." "Search and destroy" is how the late Harvard sociologist David Riesman characterized our employment of administrators.

Institutional officers might ask themselves, What are we doing to keep the good people we have? Do we keep them engaged, creative, healthy, and productive in the posts they fill? Do we offer them opportunities for advancement?

The care and feeding of administrators is a topic beyond the scope of this *Handbook*. But any institution that routinely has three or four major external searches a year, or that has had three directors of a given office over the past five, has questions to ask of itself. Your best candidates will want to know your answers.

◆

A striking fact about our most prestigious universities and better liberal arts colleges is the extent to which they bring faculty members and staff along over time and promote from within. The loyalty and talented service these institutions reap in return is no small part of their success.

The issue here is not about money. At a notably successful, multicampus community college we visited in Michigan, the greatest care is taken in the appointment and professional development of assistant and associate-level staff; deanships are filled from within that staff. At the University of California–Santa Barbara—where housing prices have made recruitment of midlevel student-affairs administrators almost impossible—an intentional strategy of staff development has been put into place. Several colleges have come to our attention that systematically identify future academic leaders within the faculty, then get them an American Council on Education (ACE) fellowship, for example, or fund their way to Association of American Colleges and Universities (AAC&U) or League for Innovation in the Community College conferences, arrange an internship under a talented mentor, and otherwise provide for their readiness for administrative leadership. Within denominational-college networks, too, one finds programs to identify and develop talent, so that a good pool of apt candidates stands ready at the start of searches.

All these examples speak to a single point: in the long run, it's more effective and less expensive to grow your own. A pattern of continual external searches may be a sign of shortsighted management.

◆

Beyond factors of cost, morale, and risk in an external appointment, there is still another reason peculiar to higher education for the nurture of internal talent: change takes time and continuity of leadership to effect. The potential problem with an outsider coming into a position is that he or she takes a year or two to learn the institution, then (for whatever reason, but all too frequently) that person is gone by the third. An able insider, by contrast, who already knows the ropes and has a longer-term commitment to the institution, can move ahead quickly with a focused agenda from the start.

The bias here, obviously, is toward support and development of your own people. Certainly there will be situations in which there isn't the talent available at home and the institution has to look outside for the expertise, leadership, or fresh perspective it needs. Smaller institutions in particular may not be able to provide the range of experience at lower levels they would want for upper-level posts. Sometimes institutions, divisions, or entire offices are simply too ingrown, and a person from the outside becomes a necessity. Even so, it is dismaying to find so few institutions with deliberate, longer-term efforts to develop talent within, and even more so to find institutions that mandate external searches even when talented candidates are available within.

Our message: Don't overlook your own people; think about what a need for external search may signify; plan ahead so that you'll do fewer searches.

Summing Up

A vacancy presents the opportunity for an institution to rethink a position and the character of person needed to make it work. How a given search is conceived should be a function of thoughtful position analysis, led by the institution's senior leadership. Prior to the start of search, too, a vacancy provides a chance to weigh institutional policies on employment, on the use of search committees, and toward the professional development of faculty and staff already in place.

These matters attended to, the appointing officer is now ready to turn attention to appointing a committee and designing the search, the topics of our next chapter.

CHAPTER 2

The Committee:
Composition, Charge, and Ground Rules

In this chapter we assume that the institution has completed the work outlined in chapter 1, has a good sense of what it wants from a search, and will appoint a committee to conduct it. We now address issues that confront the appointing officer as he or she gathers and charges a committee, then raise matters the officer and committee will weigh together to get the search off to a good start.

The Chair

The one constant behind well-functioning, successful committees, search veterans agree, is an able, committed chair. For an appointing officer, then, the place to start building a committee is with the chair. No other person will play so significant a role in the process. The chair sets the tone and pace of committee work, leads its deepening conversation about the position and pool, speaks for the committee on campus and with candidates, and is responsible for crafting final recommendations.

A good chair facilitates, motivates, and *leads*. He or she must have the full confidence of the appointing officer. The officer, knowing that the chair's work commitment necessarily will be two or three times that of other committee members, arranges in advance for the chair to have the freed-up time and staff support needed to succeed.

The qualities one wants in the search-committee chair are those sought for all committee members (good judgment, for example), plus a few special qualities: good communication and organizational skills, abilities to motivate and keep a group on track, dispatch with paperwork, skill in conflict situations, and experi-ence in institutional advocacy. The chair also must be senior and independent-enough a figure to command respect of and for the committee (and not be perceived as the appointing officer's puppet).

The time commitment of the chair cannot be emphasized enough. Read ahead in these pages and you'll see the chair planning and running meetings, preparing basic documents for the search, supervising and making reference calls, recruiting and nurturing candidacies, overseeing technology and correspondence, hosting and debriefing multiple parties, communicating to the campus and administration, managing the politics of what can be a long, bumpy process, and much more. In short, this is not just another committee assignment. Done right, the role of the chair demands time and energy supported by adequate staff and funding, all of which should be reflected in the appointing officer's arrangements for the search.

◆

Most campus parties instinctively know the importance of the chair's role and will welcome overtures from the appointing officer seeking names in nomination. Depending on campus custom, the officer may want (confidentially) to run a name or two by the president's senior advisors, the faculty senate executive committee, and key figures within the office of the vacancy before making a choice and offering the assignment.

A big mistake that appointing officers often make is to cobble together a committee and leave *it* to choose a chair—a task that nobody wants (it wasn't part of their acceptance, for one) and that someone, for better or ill, finally gets dragooned into. The role is simply too important to leave to electoral happenstance.

The chair's role is so important that we've seen instances in which the responsible vice president assumed that role herself, and still another in which a president and a senior professor worked as co-chairs throughout the search. Most appointing officers wouldn't want that level of participation in the unfolding of a search; indeed, many campus cultures would balk at it. But in high-trust climates in which all agree that much is at stake and that any appointment must satisfy all parties, thought should be given to the idea of fuller participation by the appointing officer or to a "search advisory" model of committee work.

Let's proceed with the assumption of a separate chair. When the chair has been identified and has accepted the assignment, the appointing officer and chair-designate work together on formation of the committee.

How Large Should the Committee Be?

Social scientists (and common sense) make the rule here clear: almost all search committees should have at least five members but no more than nine. Researchers tell us that a committee with fewer than five members lacks critical mass; as committees grow to 15 or 20, each person's sense of belonging and contribution falls off sharply.

Most committees, in fact, should have just five or six members, a rule of parsimony that conserves professional time and permits a speedier process. For the broad run of position vacancies—a directorship of financial aid or of summer sessions, for example—a committee of five or six is more than adequate to provide for all necessary participation and expertise. A larger com-

mittee size—seven to nine persons—would be warranted for positions of sweeping responsibility, varied constituencies, and intense politics, such as a provost or an athletic director.

A mistake of the inexperienced vice president is to say, "The vacant deanship has 14 departments and units reporting to it. I'll take one person from each, add three outside faculty, a couple of students . . . let's see, I need a committee of 19 people." This line of reasoning raises two errors. The first we have mentioned: nineteen is just too many people to work effectively as a group. The second error lies in viewing a search committee as a constituent assembly, as so many "representatives of" rather than as a specially formed group acting on behalf of the institution—which is what a search committee, unlike a committee of the faculty senate, in fact must be.

If faculty and staff in your institution are used to committees of a dozen or more and will cry "foul" or feel "excluded," a compromise of sorts is to ask individuals from (say) those 14 departments to sit as a specially convened interview group at the time of campus visits.

Committee Composition

A carefully constructed search committee is a work of art. The appointing officer and the chair want an able group of complementing talents that can work together to accomplish an institutional task. No single rule will always apply; the matter is ever situational. Here, though, are three criteria to help think through matters of committee composition, with the first two of greatest importance:

1. **Personal qualities.** The first thing an institution needs in all committee members is the quality that justifies a committee in the first place: good judgment. The best search-committee members will be savvy about people; they are discerners of talent who know and insist upon high-quality work. An institution needs committee members of personal integrity and independence of view,

people devoted to the institution even if they can be critical of it. Each should be willing to assume the assignment and be able to make time for it. As a group, the committee should have a status commensurate with the position at stake, a stature that warrants the respect and confidence of relevant constituencies. (A search committee for a provost, then, should have at least two or more senior professors among its members.) Avoid the appointment of known cranks, gossips, and egotists, who simply do not work well on *any* committee.

2. **The stakeholders**. The second broad criterion is that committee composition should reflect the interest that various constituencies have in the outcome. Faculty members, of course, are the chief stakeholders in academic appointments; they would normally comprise a majority of any committee charged with finding a provost, dean, or division chair and sit on most other search committees, given the centrality of academic affairs in institutional life. For most posts, there will be administrators, students, staff, and perhaps external parties with a stake that warrants committee membership.

A variant on this theme applies to searches for heads of larger units or offices that themselves house numbers of professionals or specialists (such as a library, student-affairs division, or university press). Professionals in these offices have an obvious stake in the outcome, plus valuable experience and networks to bring to the search. Most appointing officers seek out two or three such people, from within the unit of search, for their committee.

In searches for the dean of a major school or college within the institution (law school, arts and sciences, college of nursing), up to half of the committee might be drawn from faculty within that school—but no more than half, our correspondents warn: a deanship is a *university* appointment, and the search must not be too parochial.

3. **Templates of interest**. Using the two criteria above, the appointing officer and chair assem-

ble a "short list" of possible names for appointment to the committee.

At this point, the list can be laid against other criteria: Is it senior enough, as we asked above, to signal the importance of the appointment? Does it reflect diversity by gender and race? the interest of nontenured faculty? Does it include champions for affirmative action goals? Are there new faces, not just the same people tapped (unfairly) again? (This applies especially to faculty and staff of color.) How appropriate is the list's inclusion (or not) of students? of staff? Do we have in the mix at least two or three people with search-committee experience? How about people with access to special networks of talent that the search should tap for nominees? Is anyone in the group especially adept at personnel assessment or interviewing? And, importantly, do we have campus citizens who can keep an institutional perspective throughout the process?

Given this lengthy list of considerations, it's important for all campus parties to understand that not every possible interest can be reflected in a committee of five to nine people. Every interest may be consulted, but only a short list of available people can be appointed.

The word "available" points to a problem that arises frequently. The ablest people on campus are often already overcommitted; searches never seem to come along when there's a lull. Here are suggestions, as regulations and custom permit, for broadening the pools from which committee members are drawn:

Students. Most institutions regularly appoint students to deanship and student-affairs searches. But consider a student as a sixth appointee to that search for a director of public relations or of continuing education. The right students give and learn a lot in these assignments; if there's a learning curve for them, that's why we're here. Not infrequently, especially in later stages of a search when students get their bearings and confidence, they will observe things in candidates missed by everybody else. (Interestingly, committees with students on them tend to be better behaved.)

Support staff. The next time you search for a registrar or chief business officer, name to the committee a smart departmental secretary of senior service (not from the registrar's or business office, of course). You'll pick up a shrewd, loyal committee member and send a much appreciated signal to the rest of the staff.

Retirees. Service on a search committee can be an ideal assignment for an emeritus/emerita professor or administrator living in town. He or she can lend a sense of balance and detached wisdom to a group and may be the one person who either knows or has the time to learn a position's history. Again, a positive signal is sent to an important group.

Community figures. Consider asking to serve, on that search for an education school dean, an admired superintendent or "teacher of the year"—and build into your committee an antidote to business-as-usual. The director of nursing at your metropolitan hospital, the head of the state performing arts society, or a just-retired corporate president can each bring to a given committee unique insight. Like students and staff, an "outside" appointee may need a bit of up-front coaching to appreciate academic folkways and labor markets, but the returns can be well worth it.

Depending on campus custom, there may be faculty, staff, or student nomination or nomination by self, department, or elected body. The appointing officer and chair may themselves want to solicit directly the interest of key individuals, to assure that the eventual group displays best qualities of status, judgment, and representativeness. However it is assembled, a slate with alternatives is presented by the officer and chair to the president (or a vice president, for lower-level posts), who then chooses, charges, and announces the committee.

Up to this point we've been discussing the *who* of search committee composition; a few matters now need to be said about *how* those appointments are realized.

Appointing the Committee

The points just made may vary from the way things are done on your campus. It's helpful to isolate their key principles, however, as a check on your own practice.

1. The chair, upon appropriate consultation, is appointed first.
2. The chair and appointing officer assume responsibility, again with appropriate consultation, for recruiting and forming the committee.
3. The resulting body consists of individuals chosen for their ability and willingness to act on behalf of the institution.

Again, there are certainly other ways of approaching committee composition and appointment, and campus culture or rules can limit the officer's initiative. In institutions with a strong tradition of faculty governance, for example, and where a deanship or provost position is at stake, names may come forward by colleague election. On another campus, a senate, staff congress, or union may have a role in nominating people. In some settings, the appointing officer may be presented with faculty and staff who are not nominated but appointed to the committee. Whatever the case, the aim here has been to posit a clearer set of lines between authoritarian acts taken without consultation and a simple filling up of the committee through unit-level or interest-group acts. However accomplished, the goal is a search committee ready to work effectively on behalf of the institution.

Once the committee is identified, the appointing officer (president or vice president) needs to do two things. The first is to announce the search and committee to the wider campus, praising the appointments, providing a timeline, and suggesting how the campus will participate later. A good letter here can seal a committee's legitimacy. The second is to write a letter of appointment to each committee member. Included with the latter is often the appointing officer's formal charge to the committee (discussed below).

Upon receipt of their letters of appointment (and

a copy of this *Handbook*!), the committee is ready to begin.

The First Committee Meeting

The initial meeting of the search committee, scheduled for when *all* members can be present, often lasts a good three hours. An agenda would look something like this:

1. Introductions, acquaintanceship
2. Discussion and confirmation of the committee's charge
3. Orientation to institutional rules and legal requirements
4. Budget and staff support
5. Establishment of a search calendar
6. Committee and member ground rules
7. Communication strategies

Before the meeting, each member should receive a copy of the charge (to study) and a roster providing full contact information for each person on the committee. Each member should be asked to bring his or her calendar, paper or electronic, to this meeting. We will now take up the agenda items in order.

Introduction and Acquaintanceship

Any search committee has a lot of work and hard choices ahead. It is important that every person can contribute and be heard, and that the committee as a group can coalesce for the accomplishment of work. On larger campuses especially, people may not know one another very well or at all; on any committee, differences of rank and status need to be attenuated. A wise chair therefore makes time at the start for extended self-introductions in which each person describes his or her hopes for the search. The authors have seen search committees start their work with storytelling (horror stories from earlier searches, for example), with ice-breakers, even a prayer; any of these steps, of course, must fit campus culture. We've seen committees invite a facilitator to coach them in team-

work and decision making, to good effect. Whatever the device, the point is to help the committee get off to a good start as a group and to help members develop commitments to one another and their shared task.

In the Maricopa Community College system, former chancellor Paul Elsner once provided committee members charged with searching for a director of international education with copies of Madeleine Green's book *Internationalizing the Campus: A User's Guide* (2003). Committee members told us that this bit of common reading helped them develop a broader conception of the job and to define its essential functions more clearly.

Discussion and Confirmation of the Committee's Charge

With their letter of appointment, and prior to their first meeting, members should expect to receive a formal, written "charge to the committee," a memorandum setting forth the institution's expectations for the position and the search committee's role in filling it. Customarily these letters are prepared by the appointing officer and signed by the president. The charge itself need not be cast in stone; it should be discussed by the committee at this first meeting and may indeed be modified, after which it becomes the basic charter for proceeding.

Typically a search committee charge covers the following:

1. The title of the position to be filled and its character as the institution now views it. At a minimum, the committee should receive a job description; better yet, the committee should have a statement of the post's immediate and longer-term challenges and opportunities and of the administration's expectations for it. (This is the work described in chapter 1.)
2. A brief statement of the roles of the committee, its chair, and the appointing officer. This should include wording about when or under what circumstances the appointing officer wishes to participate or be consulted.

3. A preferred timing of the appointment, indicating (at least ideally) when the search should be completed and when the institution hopes the appointee will take up the post.

4. Any institutional sense of scope or limits to the search (e.g., internal, local, statewide, national, denominational or not, etc.) or characteristics the institution desires in the names brought forward (e.g., relating to affirmative action, national reputation, community college experience, etc.).

5. Instruction as to the form in which the committee's final recommendations are to be brought forward.

6. If a search firm or consultants will be in the picture, their role in relation to the committee.

7. A description of the search-related financial and staff resources available to the committee.

8. A reference to governmental and institutional regulations applicable to this search, including needs for record keeping.

9. The role of the committee, if any, after it submits its recommendations.

At its initial meeting, with the appointing officer present, the committee should review the charge thoroughly. Now is the time to resolve ambiguities, ask for changes deemed wise or necessary, and otherwise build a base of common understanding for the work that follows.

———————◆———————

Committee discussion of the charge often centers on items 2 and 5 in the preceding list.

As to item 2, does the appointing officer envision a role for himself or herself in recruiting or nominating candidates? Should the fact of a candidate's recruitment by the officer be known to the committee? Does the officer wish to comment or rule on internal candidacies before they go forward? Might he or she want to review the pool for adequacy at certain points? Will the officer participate in off-campus interviews? Do supplementary reference checking? If so, now is the time to say so and reach a collective understanding.

As to item 5, in what form shall the committee's recommendations be made, and what is the appointing officer's responsibility toward them? Is there a specific number of names that must be brought forward in final nomination? With what attached information, comment, or evaluation? Are they to be ranked? (this is *not* recommended; see chapter 7) designated as "qualified" or "best qualified?" Are dissenting reports in order? Must a final list include women or minority candidates? Are the committee's recommendations binding or advisory? Under what circumstances can the appointing officer reject an entire slate? or appoint a person who chose not to be a candidate before the committee (such as an "acting" administrator)? or reopen a search if the final list fails to produce a desired candidate or acceptance? Will this committee assume a role in any reopened search, or in a decision to appoint a given person on an interim basis?

Of course, not every possibility can be foreseen, and the aim is not to invent rules in advance for every imagined case. But there is need for a good set of understandings all around, so that the committee knows its role and what to expect in discharging it.

Orientation to Institutional Rules and Legal Requirements

Next, the new committee needs to familiarize itself with applicable legal and procedural requirements for the conduct of its work. The appointing officer and chair should arrange to have on hand copies of all relevant federal, state, and local statutes and guidelines, plus applicable institutional regulations and policy statements; the officer and chair may arrange briefings, as appropriate, by the institution's legal, human resources, and affirmative action officers.

Committee members are often stunned by the legal and regulatory requirements that surround their work. Indeed, in preparing this *Handbook* the authors considered including in it a primer on applicable law; but the legal environment varies so by state and institutional type that we abandoned that idea. (Sunshine laws alone could take up ten pages here . . . and *they* don't apply in a majority of institutions.) In lieu of discussion here, we have posted links to applicable websites on www.thesearchsource.org.

Our short advice is this: don't be buffaloed. Challenge claims that fly in the face of common sense. (e.g., "Each candidate in interviews must be asked the same question in the same words and in the same order.") Common sense does apply; learn what you *can* do, not just the "don'ts"; be as disciplined and consistent as possible; keep good records; and in most cases, you'll be fine.

Our cautions aside, of course you want a fair and lawful search, so do heed the briefings. A sensible follow-up step for a committee might be to ask a member or two (one of whom might be the chair) to learn fully the applicable requirements so as to be able to flag committee attention to them at key points or to know when further advice is needed. Such a step can help avoid thoughtless error and undue dependence on third-party experts. It can also help with another general rule: if a legal or regulatory mistake is made, don't ignore it, fix it. For example, if a committee member asks a candidate an illegal pre-employment question ("How old are you?"), the chair should tactfully but firmly step in and correct the mistake.

Two usual briefings at the committee's first meeting deserve comment.

First is the visit with the institution's affirmative action officer. Since affirmative action is a national endeavor applicable to most educational institutions, this *Handbook* will raise points related to it along the way. Even so, state or institutional plans vary, and court injunctions or state referenda may apply, so the officer's local report should always take precedence. As you'll learn, affirmative action is more than a set of do's and don'ts; it is a combination of goals, expectations, and sensitivities that should pervade all of your thinking about the attraction and selection of talent. You also may find, as many committees have, that your affirmative action officer is the single best-informed person on campus about the search process and can be a real asset to your work.

Next is the visit with your institution's director of human resources. Here again, you'll find the situation varies by institution. At one college, a clerk in the business office performs the function; at a larger institution, a vice president for human resources may stand ready with sophisticated assistance. In complex institutions, HR offices range from homes of enlightened good practice to hives of wrong-headed rule making. Between these extremes, you hope at least for a useful ally. Your HR specialist may be the smartest person on campus about candidate recruitment, reading résumés, checking references, and the details of an appointment. He or she also should be an expert on the institution's benefits and can be helpful as candidates ask questions about them. Take a moment now to learn about the institution's personnel policies and about how HR can help your work.

It also is important to talk with HR about what records to keep and about how to handle applications, notes, and minutes. A committee should keep minutes of its proceedings, so designate a recorder now. In most situations these minutes needn't be lengthy or overly formal; the point is to keep track of the rules you make and your decisions about candidates.

A failure to keep minutes invites trouble and conflict. What did we agree to last month about that application deadline? Whose job was it to notify Lopez? Did we eliminate Smith or not? Minutes have their archival and legal functions but above all they are a component of good committee process. As an aspect of preventive law, the keeping of minutes helps a committee state and follow decisions with consistency. It's worth starting each meeting with a check that minutes from the last meeting have correctly recorded committee decisions.

Budget and Staff Support

Next, the committee's orientation needs to cover the resources available for its work.

Any search incurs predictable costs—for candidate travel and hosting, for example, and for clerical help, advertisements, postage, and telephone. Some searches incur hard-to-predict costs: out-of-town travel by committee members to meet a candidate at an airport, for example, or to engage a consultant. Whatever, the committee needs to know up front what money it has to

MORE ON AFFIRMATIVE ACTION: A LETTER

Julie A. Sweitzer
Carol A. Carrier

If there is one thing higher education knows, it is that hiring strong faculty, professional staff, and other employees is critical to an institution's vitality. Good hiring requires good human resources guidance, and affirmative action only enhances the strength of any search.

At the University of Minnesota, the Office of Equal Opportunity and Affirmative Action's mission statement commits it to "eliminating individual and systemic barriers that inhibit individuals and groups from attaining equal access to University of Minnesota employment, education, programs, and services." That's what affirmative action is all about—eliminating barriers.

At its most basic level, affirmative action means taking steps to assure a high-quality pool of candidates representing all of the available, qualified, potential candidates. It starts with creating broad networks of relationships with potential sources of candidates in advance of any search; personal connections do remain important. Affirmative action challenges us to connect with more and different networks than we have relied on in the past. Every college that recruits graduate students and athletic coaches has invested in strategies that develop relationships to attract the best. That same energy and creativity goes far in recruiting all professional talent.

The role of the search committee is twofold. First, it serves as a front door to the institution, recruiting and screening candidates, then advancing the most promising prospects for consideration. The second role is to present the position and institution in a manner that attracts and intrigues talented candidates. In today's world, this requires clear, direct communication about the institution's values, resources, and policies—policies, for example, on spousal or partner hiring, flexible leave policies, and child- or eldercare resources available to employees, to name but a few.

Before the position is posted, a search committee must carefully review job descriptions and minimum requirements to see if they truly are necessary for the position, or whether greater flexibility would attract more candidates. Each search committee should also expressly talk about how it can best assure that all members' opinions are heard and fairly considered by their colleagues on the committee.

We all watched the University of Michigan argue successfully the value of diversity of opinion and perspectives among a student body because it enhances learning. That same diversity enhances learning and discernment about candidates for faculty and administrative positions.

We hope our advice sounds like good human resources practices generally, because it is. A quality search should incorporate these elements of affirmative action naturally. Sometimes due to a time crunch or work pressures, we choose simpler routes that may result in a competent employee, but cut short the opportunity for many potential candidates to have their fair consideration. Expediency rarely leads to excellence.

Technology has produced new tools that broaden access to information and provide easier job application methods. This has affected the role of the search committee, as more and more online resources emerge that enhance access to information about the institution. Candidates can now learn in depth about an organization through websites detailing the activities and priorities of even its smallest departments. This can lull search committees into thinking that their role in reaching out and explaining is now less important; in fact, candidates faced with so much information more than ever seek a guide to interpreting the culture of the organization. The search committee, again, acts as the front door to the institution; its effectiveness at opening that door and welcoming potential candidates is critical.

The future of our faculties and administrations is at stake.

Julie A. Sweitzer is director of equal opportunity and affirmative action, and Carol A. Carrier is vice president of human resources, both at the University of Minnesota.

work with. Committee members need to understand the rules for its expenditure and for their own expense reimbursement.

Not infrequently, committees confront a situation in which there is no set budget or only a quite small budgeted amount. A substantive issue may be at stake: when an administration charges a committee to find and land "the best librarian in the nation" and designates $800 for the task, something is awry that needs to be addressed with the appointing officer.

Just as often, the committee receives no clear guidance about what it can spend: "We have some money in the president's discretionary fund, I have a kitty for emergencies, maybe we could tap the university foundation for help . . . ," and so on. Many institutions don't budget at all for searches, we're told, because "our president doesn't like to predict bad news in the budget" or because "we can't know in advance how many searches we'll have" (despite having had three a year for the last five years) or because "the state won't allow it." Whatever the reason, a good search requires adequate funding, and it is the institution's responsibility—and the appointing officer's problem, not the committee's—to find it.

How much funding is required? Leaving aside the opportunity costs associated with search-committee service, and focusing on a search for a dean-level position, items to be budgeted for might include the following: First, in the ideal situation, the chair gets released time for his or her service, which means there is the cost of a replacement. Next comes the salary and benefits of (say) a quarter-time administrative assistant to the committee for the duration of the search (typically, five months). There also needs to be a budget for

advertising ($2,000),
committee meals and refreshments ($1,000),
candidate travel to neutral-site interviews ($10,000),
committee and candidate housing for those interviews ($2,000),
finalist visits to campus ($5,000), and
telephone, postage, and possibly, website development ($2,000).

These cost estimates (made in 2005) reflect the experience of several recent search committees. Your actual costs will vary from these, not least by the choices you make along the way. In institutions where funding will fall short of these levels, the challenges to a committee rise, and expectations for its work need adjustment.

———◆———

The appointing officer should now brief the committee on the institution's budget parameters for the post to be filled. What is the salary range? The fringe benefits? Do we help with relocation expenses, partner employment, housing and school arrangements, and the like? Committee members need to know these facts (often confidentially), not for the purpose of holding out offers to people (they never should; it's not their role), but because they'll need to know at least the general budget circumstances of the appointment when they attempt to recruit people to the pool.

Staff support is vital to the committee's work. At a minimum, the committee needs to count on the time and help of a discreet, able administrative assistant (preferably not from the office of the vacancy).

Beyond this, and highly desirable, is the arrangement we found at a number of larger universities (but applicable anywhere). These have designated an experienced, upper-level staff person, often situated in a president's, provost's, or vice president's office, to serve as *aide-de-camp* to every campuswide search committee, with such service constituting a third to a half of that person's full-time work. For a committee, as appropriate, and with the help of the administrative assistant, this person supervises office work, arranges necessary briefings, handles candidate travel, housing, scheduling, hosting, and reimbursement, oversees the committee's secure website or portal, and more substantively, contributes to tasks of pool building, résumé review, reference and credential checks, and interviewing. This person can be a superb complement to a search committee's work and a lifesaver for the chair. He or she manifests the institution's commitment to aggressive, professionally done search and to the high standards of work it takes to realize top appointments.

STAFF ASSISTANT ROLE

An efficient, organized staff member smooths the progress of a search and makes everything easier for committee members and candidates alike. The assistant's *courtesy and professionalism* are manifest in duties that include the following:

- Scheduling meetings and appointments, including arrangements for rooms, refreshments, and AV or telecommunications
- Drafting and keeping minutes
- Promptly acknowledging applications and subsequent correspondence
- Maintaining committee files and postings to website
- Handling mailings to candidates
- Organizing details of neutral-site and on-campus interviews
- Processing expense reports and tracking the committee's budget
- Completing the census check with the HR or affirmative action office
- Assisting with the closing of the search (records retention, final report, etc.)

Given the nature of the staff assistant's role, do ask for his or her observations about candidates. How a candidate treats staff can be revealing.

Establishing a Search Calendar

The steps in almost any search can be seen as a given, as is the time they take. Now is the moment, then, to identify and set aside specific times for every forthcoming meeting of the committee and to get these meetings on members' calendars. In the following paragraphs, we suggest the number of meetings that may be necessary and the approximate time to set aside for each.

The next (second) meeting of the search committee will likely occur in a week or two, and it needn't be long. (Set aside two hours for it.) The need then is to regroup as a committee, approve the public announcements and ads that will go out, learn about staff support and website arrangements, prepare a campus announcement about the committee and its search, and talk together about strategies and roles in recruitment. If a prospectus has been prepared, it too should be vetted and approved for use.

Most committees set aside approximately two months for the ads to run and a pool to be built. The third committee meeting is optional but could occur near the end of those two months, perhaps ten days before you say you will commence reviewing applica-

tions. The point of such a meeting—allow two hours for it, too—is to practice reading résumés and review the status of recruitment (more on these steps later).

Just after the announced date for application review and after members have read and rated all applications, comes a fourth, longer meeting—allow three to four hours for it—to reduce the candidate pile to manageable proportions—to perhaps 8 to 15 candidates, whose references will then be checked.

Allow two weeks for the calling of named references, upon which the committee meets again, perhaps for three hours, to hear reports on candidates and select a smaller number (five to eight) to invite for interviews, at a neutral site or by phone.

The off-campus interviews, if you elect to hold them, will likely span two full days and may take two to three weeks of lead time to arrange. Because of your own busy schedules and those of candidates (who have jobs, too), "neutral sites" may have to be scheduled for a Friday and Saturday. Once that pair of dates is identified, each committee member has to set aside that time.

At the conclusion of these interviews, committees typically select two to four candidates to bring to campus for further rounds of interviewing, tours, and receptions. Campus visits usually take place two to three weeks after the phone or neutral-site interviews; each visit can typically consume the better part of two days. Each committee member should protect time during the period of visiting and be ready for meetings with candidates and spot hosting.

Shortly after the last candidate visit, after further reference calls and collection of campus feedback, the committee needs to set aside time for a three-hour meeting to prepare its recommendations for the appointing officer. If all goes well, this should be the final meeting.

———◆———

The reason to spend time now to identify—seemingly far in advance—the date, time, and length of every meeting is that the full, intact membership of the committee is essential to its work over time. As successive meetings unfold, the committee develops a continuing, deepening conversation about the post and candidacies. How important is a PhD? Could someone from a law school do this work? How about someone from a less prestigious institution? Or with no experience on our kind of campus? Does it matter if this candidate hasn't earned tenure? On and on the questions go, but what you want is to avoid having them come up again and again as missing members return to rehash things. Nor do you want an in-and-out member to insist that his favorite candidate, voted down at the prior meeting, be resurrected. Most important, you want to count on having every person's perspective at the table as discussions unfold and key choices are made.

To save time, the committee's administrative assistant can scout out in advance the class schedules of faculty and student members of the committee and identify blocks of time that appear open on everybody's schedule. If your campus uses central scheduling software, the schedules of administrators on the committee can also be checked in advance.

Committee and Member Ground Rules

Search committees do well to devote time early to developing necessary understandings and expectations about their work. Those that follow are usual but not automatic in every case.

Participation. A first understanding is already implied: that members will give priority to the search and will participate in full in every meeting (and turn off those cell phones). If it develops that a committee member simply cannot fit meetings into his or her schedule, a replacement should be found now. Of course there will be an occasional absence; illness happens. But if a member has multiple absences, the chair should accept his or her resignation.

Homework. A second obligation of service is that each member agrees to do the necessary work of search: read and rate the applications, make assigned reference calls, and share in the hosting during campus visits. The obligation of committee members, busy people all, is to manage their schedules in ways that allow the doing of these tasks, coming as they do at predictable times.

Decision making. A third understanding is that decisions will be made by consensus. It is counterproductive to force *Robert's Rules of Order* and formal voting on the committee; a well-functioning group, guided by a skilled chair, hears all voices, waits for a sense of the group to form, articulates that, then moves on.

Private complaint. In the category of "ground rules," each member must feel responsible for bringing immediately to the committee or chair any doubts about the diligence or fairness of the proceedings. The committee should engage these concerns as they arise, no matter how "picky," and resolve them. It is far better to deal with doubt or conflict as it arises than to confront it later as an estranged member goes public with a grievance.

Confidentiality. Matters of confidentiality prove troublesome to virtually every search committee. The ethic of academe is one of free and open communication, the sharing and testing with others of ideas and information. Indeed, with most other campus committees, members are expected to report back to colleagues; committee doings, indeed, become a staple for campus gossip.

It is against strong winds, then, that search committees must insist upon totally different norms: no open sharing, no private reporting, no snippets of gossip. The overriding needs are to protect the integrity and candor of member-to-member discussion, and to protect the identity of people (including internal candidates) who have allowed you to consider their names.

———◆———

We recommend that at your first committee meeting you discuss what you mean by *confidentiality*. Can you share with the campus how many applications you receive? Will you tell colleagues whether there are internal candidates in the pool? What details of the search will be made public? By whom? Put the *shared understanding* you arrive at in writing in the minutes.

An essence of good recruitment and personnel practice is that candidates know the extent to which the privacy of their applications will be protected. In sunshine-law states, people know (because they're told) that their candidacies will eventually be a matter of public record. In all other instances, candidates will assume (and you will be assuring them it's so) that their candidacies will be held in confidence until the point that they become finalists and agree to visit campus. This is a vow that must be kept. Break it and you undermine a candidate's standing at home, and you will see your pool start to fall apart.

Members owe a duty to one another to protect absolutely the freest expression of opinion in committee deliberation. Especially in discussing individual candidates, every remark must be taken as privileged. "What you hear stays here. What you say stays here."

Our recommendation is this: in accepting committee membership, each member assumes a responsibility not to mention any candidate's name or status, or the content of any committee conversation, to any noncommittee person within or outside the institution, *in perpetuity*. Members serve on behalf of the institution, not as constituent representatives, and therefore do not engage in private reporting back in their home office or department; nor do they respond to the inevitable questions from colleagues or the press looking for gossip or a scoop. By committee stipulation, the chair should be empowered to ask for the resignation of any committee member who breaches these agreements.

Who Speaks for the Committee?

A final ground rule follows closely on the above: all public representations about the search must be made by the chair. These will concern the committee's process and the status of the search, never people by name. A rule that only the chair speaks for the committee avoids mixed messages and not incidentally protects all other members from the importuning of colleagues and the press.

DYSFUNCTIONAL COMMITTEES

After two full meetings, a committee's "personality" is usually pretty clear. Suppose the group in some way turns out to be dysfunctional—committee members who bicker, miss meetings, harbor sullen agendas, cannot agree, or a chair who fails to win the confidence of the group.

Hard as it may be, this may be a time for the appointing officer—it is his or her committee—to intervene and set things right, with steps that could include replacing members. A dysfunctional committee will sooner or later come to grief, scaring up political problems and scaring off strong candidates.

You might also consider adopting a Search Committee Code of Ethics. This is a document, sometimes used at an institutional level and often in presidential searches, that each member of the committee signs to formalize collective expectations for conduct. See www.thesearchsource.org for examples.

Communication Strategies

To forestall political problems, encourage positive regard for its process, and to build a climate of acceptance for the eventual appointment, the committee needs to think now about what, how, and to whom it will communicate during the search. The committee as a whole needs to weigh the matter and form a plan, which is then discharged by the chair.

The highest level of regular reporting is to the appointing officer, the final constituent for the committee's work. With his or her concurrence, certain other senior officers may receive periodic briefings.

For faculty, students, or staff at large, the committee may want to provide updates in campuswide periodicals, at senate or other governance meetings, by occasional campuswide e-mails, or through postings on the institution's website. Who is most concerned about this appointment? Keep those people informed about the progress of the search. Make sure they understand early, for example, about your need for confidentiality throughout the process. What you want is a perception that the committee knows what it is doing and is running a fair, diligent process. This has everything to do with the regard and welcome that the campus will have for the eventual appointee.

It is also important to have a plan for communicating with applicants. Our suggestion: the more information, the better—but in steps as appropriate. This approach might mean, for example, sending all applicants a catalog, viewbook, job description, and your prospectus. To a smaller group of semifinalists you might follow up with a mailing of the institution's strategic plan, fact book, and most recent ac-

creditation report. For finalists, budgets, minutes, speeches, annual reports, organizational charts, and the like become relevant, plus information about local real estate, civic life, schools, cultural institutions, and recreation. Mailings like these win friends for your institution and heighten candidate commitment to your process.

When you advertise the vacancy, many potential candidates will go to your institution's website to get a better sense of your campus. Take a look now at that website from an outside professional's perspective. What you may see—this is common—is a website long on information for prospective students and sports fans but short on information about the institution itself. You won't redo an entire website for the sake of one search, but consider establishing a spot on it about the search, where interested parties can learn what they need initially to apply, then later what they need to develop a deeper interest in the position. Putting at least some of the documents mentioned in the preceding paragraph on the website might save a mailing or two.

Whether by Web or mail, a communication plan like this is public relations at its best—giving people the information they need when they need it and simultaneously showing candidates that the search (and the institution) is well managed.

Summing Up

An effective search process begins with a good set of understandings, developed by institutional leaders, about the vacant position and its requirements; these were the subject of chapter 1.

In this second chapter, we examined committee size, composition, role, and leadership—matters ever subject to campus custom and politics. Once it is formed, every search committee must address its own needs—for expertise, funding, staff assistance, member time, and confidentiality—*before* any particular of the search itself is addressed.

There remains still one more committee task prior to going public with a search, to which we now turn in chapter 3.

CHECKLIST OF BEST PRACTICES

Caroline Sotello Viernes Turner

A question all search committees ask today is, "How do we increase the diversity of our candidate pool?" One of the most valuable resources for answering that question is *Diversifying the Faculty: A Guidebook for Search Committees*, by Caroline Sotello Viernes Turner (2002). Though their primary focus is faculty searches, Turner's recommendations are quite apt, and we have slightly modified them here for administrative searches. Many of her recommendations are just plain good search practice.

Before the Search

Good

- Clearly articulate the campus rationale for support of faculty and administrative racial and ethnic diversity.
- Create a search committee that is enthusiastic about and genuinely committed to faculty and administrative diversity.
- Develop and distribute a presidential statement outlining meaningful steps to achieve greater diversity within the student body, faculty, and administration.
- Incorporate the university's commitment to diversity and inclusiveness into campus and community addresses and publications.

Better

In addition to the above,

- Create a diverse search committee—composed of faculty, administrators, and students from both minority and nonminority backgrounds—that brings multiple perspectives and fresh ideas.
- Make sure that the search process is also viewed as a critical retention tool.
- Require diversity training for all administrators, chairpersons, and staff supervisors.
- Include and align a commitment to diversity in institutional and departmental strategic plans and mission statements.
- Create open lines of communication with potential administrators already on your campus.

Best

In addition to all of the above,

- Secure all resources needed to conduct a comprehensive search.
- Make sure that your campus has developed and continually audits a comprehensive plan to address commitment to diversity in every area of campus life—faculty and administrator hiring, curricular reform, student enrollment, campus activities, and the general campus climate.

- Establish and cultivate relationships with local and national minority organizations and special-interest groups.

During the Search

Good

- Explain to the committee its charge from the outset; a commitment to the racial and ethnic diversity of faculty and administrators must be a clearly stated goal.
- Critically analyze the job description and advertisement, making sure that they are geared toward inclusiveness.
- Mail position announcements to minority groups and organizations—university and local organizations such as minority alumni and local minority churches and organizations.
- During the campus visit, make sure that all interactions with the candidate are honest and genuine.
- Offer to make available a person of similar background, interests, ethnicity, or gender to give their perspective on the campus and local community climate.

Better

In addition to the above,

- Write a position description that attracts a diverse group of applicants.
- Contact by letter and phone previous faculty and administrators of color, visiting scholars and individuals who have made diversity-related presentations on campus.
- Establish a vita bank.
- Use e-mail distribution lists, bulletin boards, and other forms of technology to announce positions and recruit potential candidates.

Best

In addition to all of the above,

- Educate the search committee on, and provide opportunities for discussion about, diversity and equity issues, including affirmative action rules and regulations, hiring myths, stereotypes, and biases.
- Use personal and professional networks to seek leads to potential minority candidates.
- Advise candidates of any incentives that might be negotiable in the salary package (professional development, reduced work loads, grant-funded opportunities, etc.).
- Cover the cost of an additional campus and area visit to explore housing.

Adapted and used with permission from *Diversifying the Faculty: A Guidebook for Search Committees* (2002) by Association of American Colleges and Universities, Washington, D.C. (reprinted with author's permission).

CHAPTER 3

The Job:
Identifying Preferred Qualifications

The search committee now has its charge plus a good sense of itself, its calendar, and its terms of work. It is ready for its initial substantive task of search: to determine as precisely as possible what it will search for.

In the days after its initial meeting, basic work has to be done to draft a statement of preferred qualifications—a one-page declaration of what the committee is looking for. That statement becomes the committee's touchstone for all succeeding acts of recruitment, screening, interview, and recommendation. The lead in preparing such a draft is typically taken by the chair and appointing officer, with single or paired committee members contributing along the way. What you want is a draft ready for committee discussion and adoption at its second meeting.

The need for this work will usually be apparent from a closer inspection of the charge and job description. The charge typically deals with macro-level concerns; for its own work, the committee needs a fuller, more concrete sense of the position. The charge may state, for example, that the committee should look for an education school dean "with a K–16 perspective," but an effective dean has larger responsibilities than that, and it is to those that the committee must now look.

As for the job description, it may not have been redone in years and probably doesn't correspond very well with the charge. In any case, it typically deals with formal aspects of the position (like reporting relationships), not with what's needed in a person to do it, the

"who" question that is the committee's chief concern. Even so, a job description has value and candidates will want to see one. If it needs updating, a committee member or two might work with the appointing officer to complete this work.

The committee's task here will depend on the depth of position analysis done earlier. The greater the specificity of that analysis, the clearer become the preferred qualifications. Alas, senior administrators face demands from all sides, and many committees wind up at the table with minimal instructions from above. Be that as it may, the search committee wants to accomplish two additional things at this point: to learn for itself about the job and its fuller requirements, and through acts of listening and dialogue connect constituents of the position with its process.

Putting together a list of preferred qualifications entails three steps of analysis: of the job, of what it takes to do that job, and of who will succeed in it.

What Is the Job?

The starting point here is certainly the committee's charge and the job description, backstopped by whatever work has been accomplished by way of position analysis. What are the outstanding needs in the office? What does the institution want this office to be like five years from now? With this appointment, are we primarily trying to overcome today's problems or move to a new agenda? Both of these objectives are valid, but each points in a different direction for candidates. Is it realistic to expect in the same person abilities to "clean house in a tough-minded way" and to provide "visionary leadership"? In the largest sense, what does this job need most?

These questions, of course, are like those posed in chapter 1. As the search committee takes life, it wants to know and embrace the institution's intentions for the position, but also to form its own, deeper understanding of the position and its needs.

As an example of the latter, it is most helpful for a committee—even as it keeps its eye on what higher ups want accomplished in the position—to be aware of the daily, unalterable tasks of the job. Inevitably there will be calls to be answered, meetings to attend, students to see, reports to complete, and so on. Committee members may want to schedule time for an extended visit with the office of vacancy, to ground themselves more fully in a sense of its daily work.

A good source for information about that work may be the departing incumbent (plus any predecessors who may be accessible). Oddly, committees seldom visit a departing officer. "Once I announced my resignation, it's as though I became unclean," one told us. Committees have been known, in fact, to list a departing dean's faults, then write down the opposite of each as what they'd look for, overlooking the dozen other things that dean did well. So do visit with the departing person; you'll learn a lot.

In fact, you'll want to do all the consultation possible at this early stage: with administrative subordinates, peers, and supervisors of the position; with the president and key vice presidents; with certain faculty, students, and other constituents of the position; and, of course, with staff within the office at stake. What do these parties think is needed next and want you to look for? Most often, people are glad to be asked and more than willing to tell you what to do. People, too, tend to trust committees that ask and listen; all this activity

lays a crucial floor of credibility for later stages of the search and the resulting appointment.

In the search for answers, the chair and individual committee members might make short appointments with people most important to the search (the committee's assistant can help schedule these) and call others by phone, request opinion by e-mail, or hold an open hearing with relevant faculty and staff. As it meets with people, it flushes out early the hidden agendas lurking in various quarters. Too, it educates itself about the position in ways that will be helpful later in talking with candidates.

———◆———

What does a committee do when it pokes into an office more deeply, only to find a mare's nest of problems crying for resolution (and to which you'd never want to expose a good candidate)? Just such a situation recently confronted a search committee at a California state university, a committee appointed on the heels of a succession of short-term directors and a failed search. It decided to halt its process momentarily, worked with the appointing officer to bring in two consultants, saw to it that certain issues were addressed by the president and provost, *then*, weeks later, commenced its search, which was successful.

Situations like this won't be covered in your charge, but they illustrate an adage: a search can't solve underlying problems, only the institution can. If the last three incumbents failed in the job, before you search again, prod institutional officers to rethink the job. At best a search can be *part* of a solution; it is seldom *the* solution. The California example illustrates, too, our premise that you start with the job, not with the person.

What Does It Take to Do This Job?

Once it has a concrete sense of the position's functions and agendas, the committee then asks, What qualities of person will it take to succeed in the position as we've defined it?

In the larger world of executive search, the professionals start with the questions in the preceding section

FOUR ERRORS

When the committee has pushed to conclusion its thinking about "what it takes to do this job" and about the knowledge, skills, abilities, and traits it will search for, it will have a statement—short, practical, and realistic—that will help it avoid four common errors that search committees make:

We'll know it when we see it. The first is that the committee is looking for indefinable, even ineffable qualities in a person, which it needn't specify since "we know a good candidate when we see one." But the abilities necessary to perform specific administrative tasks are indeed knowable, and seeing can be deceiving. Failure to specify those abilities now invites every form of bias, conflict, and erratic judgment to play itself out later.

Looking for God on a good day. The second error, captured in the delightful phrase of the late Fr. Timothy Healy of Georgetown University, is that the committee is "looking for God on a good day." In your search, you're not looking for a philosopher-king, savior-president, or superstar-academic. You're looking for someone to do administrative tasks. You realize, too, in listing a page of *preferred* qualifications, that no one candidate will possess all of them, and that human performance will always be situational and hard to predict. Your hope is to find a person with strengths in enough areas to avoid harm and get a job done well.

Reversing the funnel. Error three is the myth that we'll get the best finalists in the end if we state the toughest criteria at the start. Everyone has seen these ads: "Candidates for the position must have a PhD, seven years of teaching experience at the university level, five years of administrative experience at a comparable institution or better, and publication credentials to qualify for a tenured appointment at the full-professor level." Never mind that this ad is from a third-tier university looking to hire a registrar, or that under it almost no major university president in the United States today could have been hired—*this* committee will have standards!

What's been done, though, is to limit the looking to a handful of people meeting grand but only vaguely relevant paper requirements, at the price of screening out dozens of interesting people who could bring more to the position. There are plenty of ways, at later stages, to screen people out; in fact, that's the easy part. The error is to specify up-front requirements that prevent you from talking with a full spectrum of talent at the end.

Escaping from judgment. The final error, implicit in the example just given, is that we'll somehow be clearer, fairer, and more responsible if we advertise on the basis of specific, even quantifiable ("five years experience") criteria. There are reasons, of a sort, for highly specific job requirements, such as to justify a salary before distant bureaucracies. But these put the cart before the horse. The requirements they lead to are talent-losers.

As to the notion that quantification equates with fairness, know that the entire process of search, screening, and selection rests on human judgment, yours and the institution's, the exercise of which is indispensable, legal, and should be unabashed. Why do some committees so tightly specify requirements? As David Riesman observed, "a great deal that goes on in search is an effort to escape from judgment."

(they call it "task analysis"), then ask, What knowledge, skills, abilities, and personal traits are necessary for a person to succeed in this job? Let's take each of these four characteristics—knowledge, skills, abilities, and traits—and relate them to a collegiate search for administrative positions.

As to *knowledge*, two observations. First, many committee members, especially those with less contact with administrative work, underestimate the expertise required for today's positions, assuming (as may have been the case earlier) that any reasonably smart person can handle any administrative job. But yesterday's admissions director, gifted with a ready smile and firm handshake, has long since been replaced by marketing experts and enrollment managers armed with computer analyses. Yes, any bright person *could* learn that job, but your institution can't afford an improvising neophyte. A deanship of arts and sciences, to take another example, today entails a dozen or more arenas of special knowledge, which makes relevant experience or some form of preparation all but essential.

The second point about knowledge is that the specific requirements for it vary sharply by situation and your own expectations for the task. In a small college with a one- or two-person office of financial aid, for example, the new director of that office simply *must* have expertise in every aspect of aid administration—there's no way the office can function otherwise. In a larger aid office, however, with a capable staff of underlying experts, the "knowledge" requirement for the director could be more general. Indeed, where the institution's plan is to evolve that office into something new (an Office of Student Financial Services, say), the person sought might have quite a different background still, in program management or financial planning instead of financial aid.

———◆———

This is a good point for a word about "relevant experience." A committee would be wise to look for and examine it ever so carefully during *later* stages of candidate review, but be wary about specifying in advance the what, where, or length of that experience. The reason is that you're not looking for experience *per*

se; you're looking for the knowledge, abilities, and traits to perform your set of tasks. Experience provides a means for a person to learn and display those qualities (it's the "display," or results, you'll later examine closely), but its location or length by itself hasn't much probative value.

An adage and "old saw" apply. The former is "Experience is the best teacher." True, but it isn't the only teacher, nor will it tell you what was *learned*. Committee members will soon enough come across candidates who reflect the old saw, "One year of experience, repeated five times."

Put these two together: of course you want candidates with significant professional experience in their background; you can't afford a parvenu. In searching for a senior person to head a proposed capital campaign, then, it may be wise to state as a preferred qualification that the person has played a significant role in such a campaign before, but *un*wise to specify in advance the character or length of that role or even, perhaps, that the campaign had been in a college or university.

As to *skills* (proficiency at given tasks) and *abilities* (potential to do various tasks), these should follow directly from your work of task analysis, and might usefully be of two types in collegiate search.

First, think in terms of specific administrative skills and abilities necessary to the job as you've observed and defined it. In a given position for which there is a heavy, essential paper flow, it may be highly important to find a person able to organize his or her own and other people's work. Some positions require high levels of writing ability; a few require public-speaking facility, another may require skills of quantitative analysis; almost all require facility with computers. Keep your list of preferred administrative skills and abilities short; remember, you're specifying skills essential to the person who *directs* an office, not to the office in general, and abilities germane to *administrative* performance, not to a faculty appointment or college presidency.

Often it is not difficult to come up with a long if facile list of skills and abilities. What you want, however, is the half-dozen or so that are most crucial to the tasks actually performed by that office holder. This is where drilling down to a deeper understanding of an office becomes helpful. What actual work is that director of institutional research or student accounting responsible for? Which of it has to be done by the person himself or herself? What are the performance requirements for that work? Its essential outcomes?

Another way to discern necessary abilities is to think about the implications of your task analysis. The job as you've defined it may beg for an assertive, tough-minded, decisive person; another may want a careful, even methodical person with tact and academic sensitivity; a given position at one moment needs a creative builder and at another a process-oriented consolidator; various positions may require the patient evenhandedness of a negotiator, the group-process skills of a facilitator, or the social savvy of a lobbyist. Again, what are the abilities you want? Are there any you *don't* want?

Think also about the leadership abilities needed for the position. For certain deanships, for example, there may be an expectation of intellectual leadership. For almost any administrative position, a basic, overarching leadership requirement is the ability to advance an agenda, to organize and inspire a set of people so that work gets accomplished. This ability to follow through, to describe a task and get things done on time, is crucial to a leader's effectiveness.

———————◆———————

This brings us to the *personal traits* essential to the position as conceived. Under this heading there are basic, common-denominator characteristics, independent of the position, that you'll pay attention to later in interviews and reference checking but can omit from a starting "preferred qualifications" statement. These include traits of honesty, intelligence, loyalty, tact, and willingness to work hard. You will also be sensitive, at later points, to personal dispositions, such as toward students; to attitudes, such as toward race and gender; and to personal habits.

What you do need to list concretely under this heading now are characteristics of the person *essential* to success in this position in this institution. Is it important that the person be a Methodist? Have a com-

munity college background? Be a scientist? Have an earned doctorate? Have taught at the college level? Have published in refereed journals? Be from within the state and have legislative contacts? Have a spouse who will entertain? Be something other than white and male? Have international or intercultural experience? Be an alum? Be free to travel frequently? Must the candidate be a U.S. citizen, pass a physical, be board certified, or hold a pilot's license? Write it down.

A special issue for many committees is that of specifying academic credentials for administrative positions. At one extreme, we've seen institutions reject any such credentials as necessary, even for deanships and vice presidencies for academic affairs; they risk bringing in people who lack an important aspect of the credibility they need for effectiveness in an academic community, the bona fides to enjoy the confidence and loyalty of those they would lead. At another extreme, there are institutions and state systems wherein the only possible appointee to a dean's or provost's position must be a peer of the most senior faculty, indeed be eligible for appointment at the level of full professor with tenure in a mainstream (read "arts and sciences") department of the institution. The risk—we've seen this borne out—is that much of the talent in the latter pools gets driven out by such a requirement, including most of the younger candidates, women, people of color, and interesting people from "less exalted" disciplines. The trick for committees is to define—carefully and realistically—those credentials that are truly important to success versus those that are merely the "dues" of the academy.

Who Would Be Interested?

The final step—having wrestled with the nature of the job and of the person who could perform it—is to ask, Who would be interested in taking this job? What is that person likely to be doing now? Where? Why would he or she be willing to accept our offer? What *do* we offer?

This set of questions serves to connect the position- and person-specific information you've gathered up to now with the targeted recruitment you are about to begin. It is, too, a reality check working in both directions: if you can't answer the "who would be interested" question, it may be because your earlier work of specifying the task and qualifications was too sweeping or grand (the "looking for God on a good day" syndrome). Or, if your answer to the question fails to point to specific places to recruit, again there may be a reality gap in your planning.

The lead question of this section ("Who would be interested?") helps push your thinking about potential candidates to deeper, more concrete levels. For example, at what career stage is your ideal candidate? Is this a first professional job for a recent graduate from a higher education doctoral program? A stepping-stone opportunity for an ambitious hardcharger? An end-of-career position for a veteran administrator? In other words, for whom would this job make sense professionally? The virtue of such discernment is that it deepens your understanding of whom you're looking for and points to where to begin looking.

Another cut at the "Who would be interested?" question is this: Who would want to work for, and be successful as, as an employee of the appointing officer? This is not the question (to be faced later) of what nominee that officer would accept, but a question of what candidate would be attracted to him or her as a boss. Is the officer you're advising a "hands off" manager? If so, you better be searching for someone who enjoys working autonomously; hire that person under a supervisor who micromanages and you'll be back searching within a year. The appointing officer may be a tight-ship disciplinarian, a help-oriented mentor, a person who forever never decides, a team-oriented leader, a dissembler about to retire—whatever he or she is, that's where the job offer will come from and what your nominee will be accepting or not. A rough sense of the employee–supervisor match is important because it so reflects what this effort of search is all about: engaging a person who can work effectively in a given organizational setting.

Another question to ask is this: Given what the institution is prepared to pay for this position, whom could we attract? A Pennsylvania college that offers a $40,000 registrar's salary, with modest benefits and no moving allowance, is highly unlikely to attract a person from a top-tier California university. Every search, in other words, has its realistic bounds. Acknowledging these limitations puts you a step ahead for focused recruiting.

Many committees, search veterans attest, routinely exaggerate the attractiveness of the position they set out to fill. To some members, the salary may seem alluring; all members have a certain love for their school and its locale. The challenge is to see your institution and position as an outside professional would, warts and all, and to keep that perspective as you target your outreach to potential candidates. Aim high, but with feet on the ground.

◆

To whatever extent we can now say who would be interested, what is that person likely doing now? And where? The implicit answer of many search committees, especially those that like "five years' experience," is to say in effect, "Right now our ideal person is doing just the job that we want done but is doing it somewhere else, and since we're unique, he or she will certainly want to do it here." The statement is a parody, of course, but use it as a check on your own assumptions. Will your best candidate be someone making a lateral move? Or will you target recruitment at people one step down (i.e., those with a good base of knowledge and abilities and for whom you'd be a step up in responsibility)? If you go for a lateral move, might your new office holder be bored, feel derailed in a career sense, or ever be promotable? On the other hand, you might try a lateral recruitment if your institution, compared with others, offers candidates a significant increase in salary, higher professional prestige, or other enticements.

These last questions, which mix qualities of the candidate with aspects of the job's attractiveness, help focus a search committee's attention on what it, on behalf of the institution, has to offer in the position. You are trying to recruit someone; what is it that you have to sell? Look at your institution the way a candidate would. Make a list.

Salary. Is it relatively high or low? Fixed or negotiable? Within what range? Are there opportunities for raises, bonuses, or additional income?

Benefits. Are there any of unusual quality or value? Does the position offer security? A car? A nice office? Tuition assistance? A paid sabbatical after five years?

Prestige. Does the position or institution have any special cachet? In what circles?

Special office situation. Is there a chance, because of growth, retirements, or reorganization, to mold an office or change its direction?

Institutional identity or mission. Has your institution a vision or values that would be especially appealing to certain candidates?

Institutional situation. Do you have good morale, budget balances, a supportive legislature, or positive enrollments to sell?

Other opportunities. Are there opportunities for promotion? for participation in important councils? to teach or advise students? for professional growth? to travel and attend conferences?

The community. Is housing more affordable here? Can we offer assistance for spousal or partner employment? Do we boast good community schools? Is this an attractive, safe, stimulating town or part of the country? Can a candidate find a diversity of people and cultures?

Every institution has a special profile of characteristics that make it attractive to certain people: what are your chief attractors? List them in a positive way—fairly and candidly, not defensively. They become a key asset to your search, drivers of the PR and marketing steps you'll engage in next. And they sharpen your thinking about our original question, To whom will this position be attractive?

———◆———

When the committee has completed the work of position analysis described in this chapter, the chair takes that work, including the statement of preferred qualifications, back to the appointing officer for approval. The step is more than a courtesy: the officer needs to affirm that the institution's priorities for the position (see chapter 1) are reflected in the basic documents that will now drive the search. A practical issue is at stake: an officer who doesn't approve the qualifications isn't going to appoint candidates brought forth on their basis—a search process that cannot succeed. So work to get that approval before pressing on.

A PROSPECTUS

A frequent product of the work described in this chapter is a "prospectus" for the search, a five- to ten-page document describing the institution, the position, its opportunities and challenges, the preferred qualifications, and how to apply. The detailed information in these documents demonstrates institutional thoughtfulness to candidates and helps them self-screen at the point of application. Examples of these documents are posted at www.thesearchsource.org.

Of course, you can't prepare a prospectus without the work of position analysis described in chapters 1 and 3. But if you've done that work, turn it into a document that will become a prime vehicle for attracting the right people to your pool. We write more about how to use a prospectus in recruitment in chapter 4.

For a committee at this early stage of a search, the useful thing about a prospectus is that its production forces you to do essential homework (all the visiting, and so forth), then forces a discussion leading to its approval—great preparation for all that comes next.

When the statement is approved, communicate it in a next report to the campus community. It is especially important that the campus be aware of intended changes to the position before people begin to see candidates.

Summing Up

At this point, let's look back on what's happened and been accomplished. The committee has resisted the temptation to rush ads and letters out the door and "get on with the job," and thereby avoided the big mistake behind so many failed searches: failure to do homework at the start. The search committee now holds as assets

- an early experience of collaborative work, and thereby a better sense of itself as a group;
- credibility and trust before relevant constituencies, achieved through consultation and listening;
- a good sense of the politics and special agendas that will surround the process it manages; and
- a good working relationship with the appointing officer.

The search committee, too, has in hand important products from its work:

- A final charge, negotiated and understood
- A usable job description
- A concrete vision of the job
- A statement of preferred qualifications
- A sense of who would be interested
- Clues about where to look
- A list of assets that will attract a candidate
- A prospectus about the position and search

The committee now has in hand most of the language it needs for the next steps of position announcement, ad writing, recruitment, and correspondence. It has put together, in effect, a roadmap for its search.

CHAPTER 4

The Search:
Recruiting a Candidate Pool

An injunction heard from every search veteran we spoke with was that "committees have to undertake active search," meaning vigorous recruitment. We're not sure who exactly advocates "passive search" (an oxymoron), but the behavior proscribed is clear enough: the hapless search committee that says at the start, "Let's place an ad and see what comes in."

Your committee will indeed post ads and position announcements, and they may unearth a few interesting applicants. But too much is at stake in your work to leave matters to ads and chance. Most of the top people you'd like to interest in the position are happily and productively engaged elsewhere and will not see your ad. They have to be recruited.

Your need, then, is to get your message in front of such people, intrigue them with your opportunity, and persuade them to allow you to consider their candidacy. Your object is to build a pool of qualified candidates from which you'll have a best chance of making the appointment you want. The active searching you do now, you realize, determines all. The ultimate appointment can't be any better than the talent you bring into the pool.

Recruitment Strategies

The searching you do will proceed along two lines, rather analogous to shooting with a shotgun and a rifle: broadscale advertisement and focused contacts. We'll discuss each in turn, saving for a moment the question of *how* you want people to apply, which you will need to know to do the next steps of ad placement and personal contacts.

Advertising

To get the position you're offering in front of the largest number of potential candidates at once, the place to start is with advertising your search. You do this step first because the timelines for placing various ads, having them reach people, and for response can be long.

Fortunately for search committees in academe, there's one preeminent vehicle for such advertising, *The Chronicle of Higher Education*, which is read weekly by 70 percent of all administrators in higher education and by virtually all managers, staff, and faculty in the job market or thinking of a position change. Placing an ad in the *Chronicle* is easy and quick—you can do so by Web, mail, e-mail, and fax—with full instructions found in the "Careers" section. A medium-sized *Chronicle* display ad run once can cost $1,000 to $2,000; coincident with it you should also arrange an electronic, Web-based listing for two months, at $250 a month. For further information, visit www.chroniclecareers.com.

The *Chronicle*'s website, at this writing, was attract-

NOTA BENE

This is the point to "note well" the phenomenon raised in the Introduction. In administrative search today, applicant pools tend to be just a fraction of the size they were even ten years ago. The reasons are numerous if uncertain, but the result is clear: a simple running of ads these days almost guarantees a small, disappointing pool.

Potential candidates are far choosier about the searches they will participate in. They want good work (as we said earlier), plus good information and a good process, and they want to be *asked*. Again, for whatever the reasons, good people are more reluctant than ever to read an ad and drop an application in the mail. Entry into a search these days is increasingly a negotiated process initiated by the institution or committee.

Verbum sapientiae sat—a word to the wise is sufficient.

---

ing 170,000 visitors a week. An effective strategy might be to run a display ad once or twice in the *Chronicle* itself and the same ad on its website for the two or so months of your recruitment period.

A second, necessary step at this point—it is required by law in many public systems—is to post information about the vacancy and search internally. In some institutions internal posting must precede external advertisement by a stated number of days, so do not delay this step.

———◆———

Given the preeminence and reach of the *Chronicle*, do you need to do any further external advertising? In many cases the answer will be "no." In former days, committees would run companion ads in the Sunday *New York Times* or in a metropolitan paper, but these seldom make sense anymore. The exception would be raised by searches in which your answer to the question "Where would our candidate be working now?" would indicate "outside of higher education." Your candidate business officer, development or PR person, or IT chief might presently be working in industry or in another nonprofit. In these cases, advertise in business or trade publications read by the specialists you're after, or in certain editions of the *Wall Street Journal*. If your potential IT chief might be employed by a local firm, an ad in your metropolitan daily would make sense.

Other options? Many periodicals (such as *Change* or the *Community College Journal*) will accept your ad, but their frequency and lead times make them an iffy vehicle for time-sensitive searches. Many institutions with a special commitment to affirmative action advertise in *Black Issues in Higher Education* and *Hispanic Outlook*. The *Community College Weekly* is a good bet for two-year colleges. After noting the popularity of the *Chronicle*'s website, several for-profit websites now solicit ads for higher education vacancies or will channel job seekers' résumés to listed searches. A best remaining bet will be the newsletters put out by national, regional, or state associations of admissions officers, librarians, institutional researchers, university attorneys, and so on. Many of these associations now also maintain job positionings on their websites; their popularity means you absolutely want to list your vacancy on one or more of them. People in the relevant office on your campus can identify these newsletters and websites for you.

Finding Prospects

Attention now turns to the person-to-person networking implied by the term "active search." The object here is to locate prospective candidates. Most often these are people who are busily employed elsewhere and not reading job positionings on websites or in the *Chronicle*. These are people you first must find, then intrigue, with your search.

A search consultant starts at the other end of the process from most committees. As soon as there's a statement of preferred qualifications and a good sense of what's needed, the consultant starts looking for finalists. His or her job is to bring to a search five or more terrific people who otherwise wouldn't have applied.

You can pay a consultant thousands of dollars to find those people for you—and spend every penny well in doing so—but, again, there's no mystery to what these professionals do, and you can do it yourself.

What they do is "network like crazy." They know that ambitious, mobile administrators are joiners, attenders, and contributors to multiple, special-purpose networks, and that top administrators achieve visibility within those networks. These networks (like those in academic disciplines) can be based on a variety of factors, including graduate origin, research interest, a reform movement, issue caucus, a status of gender or race, organizational office, institutional propinquity, and so on. The trick is to identify relevant networks and informants within them, then get those people to identify potential candidates for you. (A valuable asset brought by a search consultant is a deep knowledge of networks, plus a desktop stuffed with e-mail addresses and phone numbers.)

Where to begin? By all means, with the homework you did in the preceding chapter. If you're that Pennsylvania college with a comparatively low salary to offer that figures it should search locally for a registrar, you've already identified your first set of phone calls, ten perhaps, to head registrars at regional colleges. If your dean's search led you to answer the "where" question with a statement, "as an associate dean at an Ivy League institution," there are eight calls to start with. If your search for a vice president for administration prompted you to look for an "experienced administrator who knows our kind of school and is ready to move up," start with calls to vice presidents at other schools in your region, state, or conference.

A further avenue for nominations entails looking into networks within the field of specialty (library science, continuing education, financial aid, etc.). Today, virtually every administrative specialty—there are dozens of them—has an active professional society, replete with publications, membership lists, state and regional networks, websites and bulletin boards, and often a job service. Within these associations, people tend to know one another and where the up-and-coming talent can be found. Many, too, have an accrediting

NOMINATIONS

As recently as a few years ago, well-organized searches routinely generated dozens, even hundreds, of personally addressed letters to a wide range of university and association presidents announcing the vacancy and inviting nominations. This is less common today; committees tended to encounter low response rates, lower-level replies, and presidents with annoying tendencies to nominate people they hoped to *lose.* Now, most committees avoid widely broadcast letters in favor of e-mail and the phone. Search consultants feel confident that once they have a key informant on the phone, they can push beyond that "impulse to dump" to learn who's out there.

The use of formal nominations to build a pool has also tended to fade. It's an extra step, and committees know that nominations seldom come out of the blue—they've almost always been prompted by the would-be candidate. Certainly no useful distinction should obtain in later screening between presumed nominees and other applicants.

There is a certain flattery about being nominated, even a sense of permission to participate in a search, so don't hesitate to use the word in calling people you've learned about through your networking.

or certification unit that can be a valuable source of names, since it is always on the lookout for able practitioners to put on visiting teams.

How do you learn of these organizations? Ask within the relevant office on your own campus; look at the association listing in the front pages of the *Higher Education Directory*; use a search engine to find them on the Web. However you find the relevant networks, they are your indispensable source for informants and eventual candidates.

There are still more networks and sources of nominations than these; in the "Additional Sources" box on page 39 we describe several more you would do well to tap into.

———————◆———————

As you call within professional networks, you often won't get very far by simply asking busy people to help you find the director you want, or by asking generally for them to "suggest names." Instead, tell them that you are looking, for example, for "an institutional researcher who understands Southern Association accreditation and is a specialist in assessing learning outcomes," and you've got a better shot at bringing a name to mind.

Prospect calls are an important part of the affirmative action you are taking. Be assertive in asking informants for help in identifying good potential candidates who are women or persons of color.

An intelligent use of e-mail can make your calling more effective. E-mail addresses are easy to get; before that cold call, send potential informants a two-paragraph message introducing yourself, describing the search, and saying that you'll telephone. (Sometimes you'll get a message right back with a name or two!) On the chance that you might find a personal connection with the nominator or potential candidate you're about to call, consider conducting an Internet search on her.

Sometimes vice presidents and deans are reluctant to suggest as candidates their best assistant or associate. Your creativity can circumvent that barrier. A community college looking for an admissions director phoned the college counselors in a dozen of its feeder high schools and asked, "Who are the sharpest assistant

directors of admissions who've visited you lately?" It soon had a list of twenty names, including four who garnered multiple mentions; called them; and got several to apply. (Its calls to the counselors earned it valuable points back in the schools, too.)

When you do reach an informant in a network, a good idea is to decline politely his or her offer to contact someone for you. As any good salesperson knows, the sure way to know a call is made the right way is to make it yourself. Do ask whether you may use the informant's or nominator's name in introducing yourself to the prospect.

———————◆———————

To a committee member reading this far, "active" search sounds like a great deal of telephone work. It is. But committee members shouldn't be doing most of it themselves. The appointing officer, senior administrators, an assistant to the president or associate provost, even the president or chancellor (for senior positions) should do some of this calling for you. All have contacts, discretionary time, and a stake in the outcome. Thus supported, committee members might spend more of their own time making follow-up phone calls to prospects as names turn up.

The difficulties of recruiting a good pool today underscore a real weakness in the way so many institutions approach search. A search committee, no matter how talented, seldom has the background, time, or wit for heavy-duty recruiting, which is why, more and more, search consultants are on the scene. Given that weakness and absent a search firm, institutional leaders *must* commit personal time and office resources to the recruitment function, with first responsibility being that of the appointing officer. The committee and its chair should play every apt role in recruitment, but it is the institution itself that must see to the strength of the pool.

Prospects into Candidacies

Prospecting for names is half the battle in recruitment, but it is not the end game. You want to convert the best people you've identified into candidates in your search.

ADDITIONAL SOURCES FOR PROSPECTS AND NOMINATIONS

In addition to position-specific associations, there's another set organized around institutional type. Is your institution Lutheran, devoted to liberal education, and located in Virginia? A land grant campus that's part of a state system? Such descriptors can lead you to a number of associations or consortia that your college probably holds membership in, each of which has networks you can contact. Your president's office can give you a list of such memberships your institution holds.

You may also be able to locate special networks related to the position's preferred qualifications. For example, your dean's search committee may be eager to find candidates with experience in collaborative learning or writing across the curriculum or who will want to transform teacher education or implement a language-proficiency requirement. There are indeed particular networks of people devoted to each of these causes. You can locate them through contacts within your own faculty, by checking with editors, meeting planners, foundation officers, and the like, or by calls to "generalist" associations like the Association of American Colleges & Universities and the American Association of University Professors.

Those same approaches to inquiry can lead you to still another set of networks, those devoted to talent identification and development among women or people of color. The American Council on Education's Office of Women and Minorities (and its allied ACE Fellows program) can be a good source for nominations, as can leadership programs such as AASCU's Millennium Fellows institute, the HERS summer program at Bryn Mawr, programs of the League for Innovation in Community Colleges, and Harvard's IEM and MDP programs. On the Web you'll find a number of good sites devoted to minority and women's advancement; we provide links at www.thesearchsource.org. Enlist the help of key parties on your campus, including the affirmative action officer, for further leads, especially within your state. More generally, make a practice of asking every informant from every network you reach to think specifically about women and minority prospects.

A related way of identifying specific talent is to tap into the handful of leadership development programs and institutes alive in higher education today; we've already mentioned those at ACE, AASCU, Bryn Mawr, and Harvard. Find links to others at www.thesearchsource.org. In your own state, chances are there exists a "center for the study of higher education" at a major university (there are upwards of 140 graduate programs, plus another 100 with a student-affairs orientation); they can often provide leads to graduates with backgrounds relevant to a range of midlevel administrative positions.

That process usually begins with a call to your nominee or prospect. That call is easier to make than most people imagine. The person you call may be flattered and will usually hear you out. (Search consultants find that at a given moment a fourth of all administrators are entertaining a job move, and another fourth can be intrigued if approached correctly.)

Since this first call is probably to his or her office, ask whether it's convenient to talk for a few moments; introduce yourself, briefly describe the opening, and say you'd like to e-mail the person material about the institution and position. (Your prospectus works best here.) A bit of enthusiasm on the phone helps. So will a reasonably deep knowledge of the position and its opportunities (a product of your earlier homework); honesty about its challenges will be appreciated. If participation in the search can be confidential, stress that. Schedule a follow-up phone appointment for a few days after the materials have been received. People are usually willing to at least look at what you send, and by the time of that second call they've had time to get themselves intrigued.

Not infrequently, it takes more than a call or two to get a good person to commit to your search. Potential candidates may want more information from you, time to make inquiries for themselves, time to talk with family and advisors, then still more time to think it over. Matchmaking takes patience; questions of "fit" are necessarily two-way. Your job is to stay in touch, provide honest information, and show respect. Even as you "sell" your institution and position, you know that the strongest pool will consist of informed, self-motivated candidates.

Search professionals work hard to bring excellent people into the search and to keep them there. After a prospect decides to apply, call and thank him or her for that, and send another piece of information or two. Later in the search, call again, describe the search's status, and ask if you can send a copy (say) of a new document that just became available. Chances are good that your three, five, or eight "special recruits" will compose the heart of your semifinalist pool. You want them to feel good about their participation and ready for the next step. You want to bring forward in your search candidates who can and will say "yes" to your future offer.

One way to show respect is to be mindful of a candidate's need for confidentiality. Ask if you should use a home address, private phone line, or confidential e-mail account in communicating with them. Do not send big envelopes stamped PERSONAL AND CONFIDENTIAL into a prospect's office.

The Application

What will it mean for your search to have a person "apply" for the position? What is it you'll ask interested professionals to tell the committee about themselves?

Happily, prevailing practice here has changed, much for the better, in what search committees typically ask of applicants. In days of yore, following a hundred or so general words about the position and institution, applicants in ads were usually asked to send the committee "a current vita and three letters of reference." College transcripts and a credentials file were sometimes requested, too, and then there was the six-page application form from the personnel office asking for "mother's maiden name" and leaving a line each for "experience" and "reason for leaving." Sometimes committees asked for an essay on, say, one's philosophy of education.

The shortcomings of that approach for an administrative search are all too apparent. Committees want to screen on the basis of specific "knowledge, skills, abilities, and traits" related to their position, but instead receive academic vitae that give little hint of what a person has been responsible for or accomplished administratively. Letters of reference—candidate prompted and vetted—are uniformly glowing. Transcripts and candidate-managed credentials files have just as little probative value. Absent information of value, search committees are left without rational bases for screening the pool down to the dozen or so most interesting candidates.

The approach fails, too, on practical grounds. Most administrators these days do not maintain credentials files. Potential candidates resist asking colleagues for letters of reference because doing so announces their job search. Their colleagues, in turn, resist writing letters of reference because they don't believe in them or fear legal consequences. A too-complicated process at the front end—getting letters, completing a form, degree verifications, writing an essay—discourages entry into the search, especially on the part of busy people.

Better Practice

The reason practice changed, then, was that committees wanted better, more germane information from candidates—and candidates wanted to give it to them. Here are five perspectives on an application process that will serve both parties.

Better Information for Candidates

The process should start with better information in the hands of prospects. A problem often is that people apply on the basis of the skimpiest of information (what's in a *Chronicle* ad), therefore little they send comes tailored to your setting or questions.

A better start, then, would be to run ads announcing the position, even touting the opportunity a bit, then inviting prospects to e-mail or write the committee for more information. The ad would not contain directions on how to apply. By return e-mail you would send your prospectus, or in any case information on the institution, the position, the search, your preferred qualifications, the salary range, and how to apply, along with an encouraging note. We noted with interest one recent ad in the *Chronicle*, from a Midwestern university, that gave only the name of the institution, the position, and a Web address.

The point, again, is that you're looking for candidates to apply on the basis of good knowledge and forethought, and who can be responsive to your issues. With good up-front information, candidates can self-screen, saving you (and them) from inappropriate applications.

Request tailored information. A reasonable burden can be placed on applicants at this early stage to provide the committee with information about his or her knowledge, abilities, and accomplishments relevant to the position as described. A functional résumé, detailing administrative experience and accomplishments, and a two- to four-page letter responding to your preferred qualifications can do the trick. Asking for this step of initial work can heighten the commitment of genuinely interested candidates, and appropriately discourage others, without overwhelming the applicant or committee.

As for those essays and application forms, forget them. Remember, at this point your best recruits are not job supplicants. Their entry into your search may mean no more than readiness to begin a process in which applicant and committee agree to learn more about one another in search of a fit. Anything you ask of applicants at this stage has to seem appropriate, respectful, and doable with dispatch.

Forget letters of reference. There's no role for letters of reference at this stage of the process, maybe ever. As universal experience testifies, such letters aren't probative, so do the entire academy a big favor—save a thousand hours of professional time—by *not* asking applicants for letters of reference. "The telephone and lawsuits made the device obsolete," one dean told us. His recommendation (and ours, too): "When it's time, get on the phone for *private* conversations with people you sense know the candidate's work best."

Ask only for what you need now. The process of eliciting information from candidates should be driven by a sense of your committee's stages of review, with different pieces or levels of information needed only at successive points from smaller and smaller numbers of people. At the start, then, when only initial gross screening is contemplated, the information requests you impose should focus on learning who the apparently most capable people are, and no more; you don't need now, as you may later, confirmation of degrees, transcripts, salary histories, and so on, so don't ask for them. You want an initial application that takes no more than an hour or two for a busy professional to complete, and you want that time to be devoted to questions important to you at this stage.

Be candid about salary. Harkening back to a point made earlier, be as up-front as possible with prospects about issues of salary and benefits. The frequent statement "salary negotiable" makes trouble for committees and can raise hard feelings down the line among candidates who feel misled. If the job pays in the $80,000s, say so. That figure will attract many good people who are paid less, and save the time of other people for whom it would not mean advancement.

Diffidence on the point comes in part from notions that "gentlepersons don't speak of money" (really?) or from institutional craftiness in hoping to land someone good (like, say, a woman) who might sign for less. As a search committee, you're not in charge of paying people or of salary negotiations; still, strive for the sake of fairness to bring forward all the candor you can about matters of compensation. If there's a minimum salary, or a range, state it; allow the expression "salary negotiable" in your materials only if it truly is, and significantly so.

An Application Package

With some sense of these principles, we're ready to put in place the elements of an initial application. Here are three elements you might require as a package:

1. **A functional résumé.** The résumé should list all the usual information, including details of faculty work (for academic-affairs positions) and, most important, functional detail about relevant administrative experience (e.g., name of position, dates held, responsibilities, people supervised, accomplishments attributable to candidate, etc.).

2. **A substantial letter from the candidate.** Addressed to the committee chair and two to four pages in length, this should state the candidate's interest in the institution and position and speak to the committee about his or her experience, abilities, and accomplishments in relation to the preferred qualifications. What special skills or interests might he or she bring to the position? Tell us about them. Do not convert this to an essay; administrators do not write essays, they write letters, and you want to see one.

3. **A short list of key references.** Ask at this point, too, for a short list with the names and phone numbers of the five people best acquainted with their work. Make it clear to applicants that these references will be called only at a later stage of the search, after their candidacy has gone forward, and then only with the applicant's foreknowledge. This third application element may not be strictly necessary at this point, but the list itself can be revealing and having it now saves time later.

The tripartite "application" proposed here meets tests of job-relatedness, ease of accomplishment (for

able people), appropriateness to the stage of search, and utility for the committee. Its parsimony and confidentiality (only the candidate, no other person, need know or do anything at this stage) will be welcomed by good prospects.

The Application Period

How long should a committee keep the application process open? How tight or far out should it set the date for receipt and review of applications?

No hard-and-fast rule can apply; how much time does your committee have for the entire process? A November start presents a different situation from an April start if the successful applicant is to be in place by July. As a general rule, never stint on any steps at the front end of a search (the position analysis, consulting with people, and above all, the pool-building); it is easier to make up time later than early mistakes. It would surely be a mistake, as we saw in one search, to allot three weeks for applications and three months for all the rest; arguably, those proportions should be reversed. (The search in question failed.) Among other problems, an abbreviated application period will lead some potential candidates to assume that yours is a *pro forma* search, with an appointee already selected.

Other things being equal, then, and given the time it takes to network, get the word around, and entice people into your pool, allowing eight or so weeks for recruitment and receipt of applications makes sense.

———◆———

In days of yore, legal minds persuaded many institutions to impose absolute application deadlines ("Applications received after 4 p.m. CST, April 2, 2005, cannot be considered."): somehow a time certain would be "fairer." At least it was uniform. But horror stories circulated of carefully recruited candidates subverted by the mail service, of the perfect candidate unearthed a day beyond the deadline who could never be considered, or of a good "solution" appointment that couldn't be made because that person hadn't formally applied on time.

Given these circumstances, and where regulation permits, a different practice is now recommended. The date set by the committee is not that of an absolute deadline for consideration, but that on which it will commence review of applications. The approach puts candidates on notice as to when materials should be submitted, while leaving options open to the committee for later stages of search.

Beyond questions of date, must a person formally "apply" to qualify for committee consideration? In application-deadline institutions, most of them public, the answer can be "yes"; indeed, as an attorney will tell you, there is a whole body of law on what constitutes an "application." But in other institutions no such concern arises. What this allows a committee to do, especially for a top-level position like a law school deanship, is court senior persons over time, to keep as "prospects" a few special people the committee has tentatively intrigued with the position but who won't risk formal candidacy now for fear of disclosure. Accommodations may be necessary to keep prospects on the line till later stages of the search, but at some point they will have to declare and provide you with access to information and references.

Paper or Electronic?

Until recently, virtually all searches assumed that candidates would file written applications by mail on real stationery. Today, there is a strong shift to all-electronic searches. Applicants file their materials as e-mail attachments; these are placed on a secure website or portal (using Adobe Acrobat or the like to retain formatting) with access limited strictly to committee members. The advantages for candidates are ease of applying and 24/7 access to materials on the part of committee members, who no longer must trek to a distant office to read files during business hours only. Additionally, when search files are so organized, a search secretary can easily send acknowledgments, updates, and decision letters to candidates via their private e-mail addresses, which you elicit from them.

The worry here, as always, is about the protection a website or portal can afford to your confidential process. Computer experts can help your committee construct a secure, double-password-protected site; it may be that an outside, fee-based server will have to be used. And, just as there were risks to confidentiality in paper-based searches (files could be breached, papers left unattended on desks, etc.), so with electronic search, committee members must take care not to leave passwords around, mention candidate names in regular e-mail, print résumés to an untended printer, and so on.

Internal Candidates

This *Handbook*, in chapter 1, already raised the advantages of promotion from within: the institution knows better what it's getting, continuity is served, loyalty evoked, and it can be more cost effective in the long run.

From a search committee's standpoint, finding a good internal candidate early on, a person who proves capable of appointment, can save the time and complication of external search. It can save a committee, too, from the vicissitudes of a search that mixes internal and external candidates. As soon as you turn outward for talent, insiders may assume rejection or slight, while outsiders, spotting internal candidacies, may assume the process is rigged and shy away. Of course there are successful searches that mix internal and external candidates, but they labor under a burden of constant explanation.

Search committees often have an implicit bias against internal candidates, whether from the ravages of familiarity (or unfamiliarity!), or an assumption that people outside must be better than their own, or from a sense that picking an insider is a "cop out" to "rigorous search." But consider: promotion from within is the norm in American higher education in the replacement of administrators. Research done two decades ago by Kathryn Moore, then at Penn State, showed that 55 percent of the thousands of mid- and line-level administrators she surveyed had been promoted from within. In doctoral-granting institutions, that figure rose to 63 percent; at smaller liberal arts colleges it was still 52 percent. Internal candidates were the choice in 59 percent of searches for academic affairs administrators, in 62 percent for student-affairs positions.

Contrary to what many search committees believe, there is no generally applicable law that demands external search. If a committee in consultation with the appointing officer chooses to assemble an internal pool and make its choices from within, it may do so. If the committee and appointing officer (or the latter alone) choose, without further search, to promote an "acting" to a position, that also can be done. These two statements do need qualification: in your institution there may in fact be a regulation or reason that prohibits either or both of these steps, as we'll note in a moment. But a general rule applies. In search, don't assume without checking that any next logical step is impossible.

"Internal" search needn't be restricted to a single campus; indeed, the approach makes special sense in large, public systems like a multicampus state university or a metropolitan community college district. Looking for talent within a system can bring candidates who already know its ropes and who may not bring with them significant issues of relocation, benefits, or cultural adjustment.

———————◆———————

Under what circumstances might a committee decide to look internally first? Or go outside? Or open the door to all comers from the start? Here are five factors to weigh:

Availability. Are there credible internal candidates with an interest in the position? If not, the committee should commence external search immediately. How does one ascertain whether there are internal candidates? By campuswide posting of the vacancy, by personal inquiries, then by waiting a stated interval to see who steps forward.

Timing. External search entails much longer timelines than a review of internal candidates. For a vacancy arising in fall or winter, that won't be a problem. For one arising in April or May, where a replacement must be in

the position by July, it's a very big problem, one that would point a committee toward intensive search for inside candidacies (or lead the institution to appoint an "acting").

Position level. A distinction often must be made between mid- and senior-level positions. That is, a strictly internal search may be appropriate for a director of residence halls but inappropriate for a provost, or apt for a comptroller but not a deanship. In the case of both the provost and dean positions, the positions' constituencies are broad, the stakes are high, and politically the expectations for a broadest review of talent are high. In both cases, people may welcome an eventual inside appointment, but they want that person's credentials tested against a national field. Only a full search process, given this expectation, can legitimate so crucial an appointment.

Affirmative action. A further reason for opening external search may be that you simply won't find inside the numbers of women or people of color you need to help meet affirmative action goals. Your affirmative action officer should have a workforce analysis that can help you decide whether a requisite "affirmative pool" exists to proceed internally. These data might be secondary to whether your own internal recruitment in fact turns up women and minority applicants.

Other regulations. In public institutions especially, search committees confront a variety of regulations that may decide the inside–outside question for them. Any vacant position above grade-level x or salary level y, for example, may have to invoke a "national search."

———————◆———————

If circumstances permit or demand, how should a search committee proceed internally? "Active search" for internal candidates entails straightforward steps: a position announcement is published or otherwise circulated as widely as possible; committee members themselves can prompt nominations or candidacies via personal contacts; the appointing officer, other administrators, and key faculty can be asked to come up with names; and direct inquiries can be made, perhaps by the chair, to potentially qualified individuals, especially to people within the office at stake. Once a small pool is assembled, steps of inquiry and interview follow in normal course as described in the next chapters, until you see if you have a person or persons who meet your preferred qualifications (from chapter 3) and can be recommended for appointment.

A creative internal search can raise an alternative opportunity, namely to recommend investing in the professional development of an otherwise able person so that he or she can be ready for a position within months. This works best for the more "generalist" positions for which personal ability and traits count most, with specific knowledge a secondary concern. A bright, committed, ready-to-advance faculty or staff person, for example, could be recruited for a position in spring and sent off for a summer of study, visits to other campuses, institute attendance, or an internship at a peer campus, thereby to gain at least enough knowledge and perspective to start effectively by fall, with provision then for a mentor or coach—all for a lot less than the cost of a national search.

It is doubtful you'd invest such an effort in a newcomer from outside: the approach looks to the intentional development of internal human resources. It's a step less risky than bringing in an outsider. It's an approach that can be used to advance women and minorities from within the institution. It realizes institutional mission more fully by placing alongside "student development" a parallel concept of "administrator development."

———◆———

Three last thoughts on the matter of internal candidates: First, while our treatment here of internal talent has been positive, there are whole institutions, and units and offices within them, that are simply too ingrown. External search, time and risks notwithstanding, may be necessary to bring fresh talent and perspective into the campus mix.

Second, have no part in a fake search. A fake search

is one in which the appointing officer and "everybody" else knows in advance who or what kind of person will get the appointment, with the committee and "search" put out as window dressing. If a certain person should or will be named anyway, get them appointed now. But play no role in a sham that induces false expectation and wastes countless hours of committee and candidate time.

Third, a search with internal candidates will, as we've said, raise questions or suspicions in the minds of potential candidates from outside. If your search is indeed open, you'll need to find convincing ways to make the point without being defensive. The presence of insiders in a search, for example, may be represented as showing a depth of internal talent and loyalty and as testimony to the position's attractiveness.

The Acting

A tough situation for many search committees is the presence and possible candidacy of an "acting" head of the office. There are few rules beyond sensitivity and common sense to guide you here in a situation that is often awkward.

Chances are the "acting" agreed to assume the position's duties on short notice, perhaps before he or she was fully prepared for it. Implicit promises may have attached to performance of those duties, or (often unfairly) the person may have been told in advance that he or she could *not* be a subsequent candidate, no matter what. The acting, out of institutional loyalty, may have put in a year of 70-hour weeks to keep an office afloat. A sense of gratitude may be in the air. And what will happen to this person if an outsider is brought in? No one seems quite sure. To boot, there's a good chance the acting, who may have been an assistant in the office, is a woman or person of color, a status you may want in an appointment.

How might a committee deal with this situation? Consider that prior to forming this search committee the appointing officer had three options:

- Option one was to find the job performance of the acting compelling enough to appoint him or her outright to the position. Given the existence of your committee, that obviously didn't happen.

- Option two was to find the acting's job performance so disappointing that under no circumstances would the officer name the acting to the position. If the officer so decides, from the committee's standpoint there isn't a viable candidacy, and it moves on with its search. (This same result, without reflection on job performance, may come from a prior "no candidacy" stipulation.)

- Option three was for the appointing officer to find the acting's performance good enough to warrant consideration for appointment, but not so compelling as to dispense with wider search.

The committee has a potential problem, then, only in situation three. If that be the case, the chair might want to pay a courtesy call on the acting, to introduce the search and invite candidacy. The acting, in turn, may choose not to apply, which ends the matter. Or he or she may choose to declare for the position only later.

If the acting decides to apply at the start, should the search committee proceed right away to a decision on that single candidacy? This step is taken on occasion, always with the concurrence of the appointing officer, partly out of consideration for the acting and partly, from a committee's standpoint, to unfetter subsequent search. (Of all internal candidacies, that of an acting can most scare off outside applicants.) There are arguments, of course, against the step: it may be unfair to other potential applicants, may violate affirmative action or other regulations, and may foreclose other sources of talent for the position.

———◆———

Sometimes an acting will be *so* popular and well known externally that his or her presence in the search will scare off too many others for the search to succeed. In that case, a complete, quick-time review of the acting's candidacy may be in order. Have the acting write a full

letter of application, go through extended interviews, stand for questions at public meetings, undergo thorough reference checking and background review, with all the resulting evidence compiled and presented for decision within three weeks. If positive, make the appointment; if less so, the candidacy is dead and your search, now unencumbered, proceeds.

Other than early consideration, should the candidacy of an acting receive special treatment in later stages of a search? Search experts argue that, no matter who, all candidates should be treated alike. (All should be treated *well*.) Following this rule, the committee would not, for example, invite to interview any acting or internal candidate whom it had already determined could not be appointed. An accommodation committees sometimes make, especially in more colleague-minded institutions in which an acting has served well and now risks applying, is to bring, if it is plausible to do so, that person forward to the interview stage. Whichever the case, honor to the fullest any application from an acting or other inside candidate; colleagues will care very much about (and remember for a long time) your "fairness to George" or "how the committee treated Maria." Remember, too, that if an inside person applies, that fact is entirely confidential . . . indeed, in making a progress report to the senate, for example, the chair would decline to disclose the presence or absence in the pool of internal applications.

An anecdote captures the spirit of the above. In a recent provost search, an admired but unappointable interim applied. The committee—friends of his all, some for 20 years—decided not to grant him an interview. What it then did was send a delegation of three senior members to convey the decision personally, laud his service and colleagueship, and promise that nobody else on campus would ever know of the application or decision. That interim returned to the faculty with head held high.

In reviewing internal candidates, don't lose track of the job analysis and preferred qualifications the committee developed earlier. Claims of friendship, compassion, or familiarity tend to push aside analytic thinking. But the job specifications you've worked hard on are as relevant now as ever.

Summing Up

The most important points made in this chapter are that an eventual appointment cannot be better than the talent you recruit into your pool now, and that getting the pool you want demands active steps of recruitment. The chapter's lengthy sections on "focused contacts" and "making the calls," which draw heavily on the experience of search professionals, aim to help you build the kind of candidate pool from which a top-notch appointment can be made.

In this chapter we also made the argument that you'll need to fine-tune your application process to realize from candidates the more focused information you'll want for the rational screening of candidates— the topic of our next chapter. Closing sections of this chapter raised for thought the special sensitivities you'll need for dealing with the presence (or not) of internal candidates and an "acting" in your search.

SEARCHING IN STUDENT AFFAIRS

This *Handbook* has discussed differences in search by institutional type, but searches can also vary significantly by position. Today, there are more and more specialized middle- and senior-level administrative positions in higher education. While we don't address each of these positions, committees instinctively know that there will be a difference between a search for a head librarian, a vice president for enrollment management, and director of the campus recreation center.

As administrative work becomes more specialized, professional associations and publications have developed in support of them. As an example, we highlight searches in student affairs.

On many campuses, the student-affairs division has the greatest number and variety of middle- and senior-level administrative positions. At most colleges and universities, student affairs is responsible for areas like admissions, financial aid and scholarships, registration, residence life and dining, recreation, orientation, health care, counseling, disability services, career services, tutoring and academic support, retention programs, women's centers, students of color centers, GLBT centers, intercollegiate athletics, student conduct, Greek affairs, student unions, student organizations and government, judicial affairs, international students, and campus police.

Given this, a student-affairs division conducts many, many searches, usually at three levels:

1. **Entry level.** An MA is usually required. Much of the hiring here is done at the national conferences of NASPA (National Association of Student Personnel Administrators) or of ACPA (American College Personnel Association) or at a number of regional job-search and placement conferences. The reputation of the candidate's graduate program is highly influential. Residence-life jobs dominate at this entry level: at the 2004 NASPA conference, over 500 applicants went through the job service, with 60 percent of the available positions in residence life.
2. **Midlevel.** For program head or coordinator positions, more traditional searches are the norm: some interviewing or networking is done at conferences, campus visits are involved, and graduate degree(s) and fairly extensive experience are expected.
3. **Senior level.** For directorships, a PhD is usually required, search firms are increasingly in evidence, campus visits are intense, and breadth and depth of experience are givens.

From experience, the literature, and our focus groups, we learned the following about the current state of searching in student affairs:

- The student-affairs profession is becoming increasingly feminized. Eight out of ten dean of students positions (or equivalent) at University of California campuses are held by women. One of the challenges for student affairs is attracting and retaining men.
- Diversity continues to be a major focus in searches for mid- and senior-level professionals; student affairs is often the most ethnically diverse area on a campus. When a campus wants to demonstrate its commitment to diversity, student affairs is often a first area that is looked to, given its visibility before students and the wider community.
- While student affairs nationally is a large, complex network of professionals, it is at the same time a small community where networking, one's professional reputation, the reputation of one's graduate program, and perceptions of one's institutional employer can positively and negatively influence the career of an individual.
- The culture of willingness to "work long hours for low wages" is changing in student affairs. Young professionals are asking for salaries equivalent to others paid on campus and for more balance between their professional and personal lives.
- Student affairs is often the place that senior administrators try to place partners of faculty whom they are trying to recruit.
- For mid- and senior-level positions, interviews for student-affairs positions tend to be multiday, intense, and exhaustive. They also tend to privilege extroverts.
- Students play a much larger role here than in searches for other positions on campus. Students understand that they interact more extensively with student-affairs professionals than other administrators, and that these professionals have significant effects on the quality of their out-of-the-classroom experiences.
- In student-affairs searches people recognize that skills and experience acquired in one area of the field are often transferable to another.

Some tips for improving searches in student affairs:

- Include students and take their input seriously. When possible, schedule students to meet candidates without other staff present.
- Pay attention to the hiring cycle, particularly with entry-level positions, and to the movement of people around the country or in your region.
- Be sensitive to candidates during campus visits; use their time wisely.
- Use all of your networks and professional associations during the recruitment process.
- Consider growing your own talent, especially men and staff of color, by getting students involved early on in student-affairs offices and activities.
- Include faculty and staff from academic units on student-affairs search committees. This increases understanding and builds bridges for collaboration.

CHAPTER 5

The Screening: Identifying Talent among Applicants

As the date for application review arrives, a week of intensive reading lies ahead for the committee. Members will now cull through what seem daunting piles of application materials to locate candidates of highest promise. In this chapter, we show how the committee can screen a hypothetical set of 60 applications down to 6 or 8. It's a task that demands care. These are choices about real people, with candidates and your campus alike trusting your judgment.

Initial Steps

Has your committee's assistant acknowledged receipt of all applications? Conveyed a time schedule to applicants? Sent them a packet of information to enhance their interest in your institution and search? Good!

Another check important at this point (it is often mandated) is to ask your HR officer to run an affirmative action "census" on your applicant pool. What are the number and percent of women candidates in it? And persons of color, so far as can be known? When you have these data, ask this question: Are we *satisfied* with the composition of our pool? An institution that is determined to identify women for the position will not be happy with a pool of 60 that contains only three marginally qualified women. At this point, you have the option of reopening recruitment until you achieve the pool you need.

Not incidentally, while such a check can be useful at this point, search professionals would never rely on it; from day one they continuously monitor a developing pool for affirmative action and for quality. How many of the nominees who have said yes to recruitment efforts have actually applied? An alert appointing officer

and chair never wait to the end to see what their set of applicants looks like. They work from the start to build a robust, no-surprises pool.

Assuming the pool seems robust enough, proceed with your screening. Save your census, though; you'll want its data for later analyses.

Getting Ready

Another preparatory step—this is an option that some committees unwisely skip—is a search-committee meeting a week or two before the application date. There are two points to this meeting. One, after not having met for several weeks, is to regroup, discuss the pool as it has emerged, and note any last-minute recruitment needs. Two, the chair or another committee member has been asked to prepare a form for the rating of applications; this is where it is tested and approved for use. The substantive task of the meeting is to receive coaching on résumé reading and then, using the new form, to rate and discuss three actual applications.

The form itself is relatively easy to prepare and is built around your preferred qualifications. If you have a dozen qualifications, list them in short form down the page, with cells across the page for rating a candidate 1 (low) to 5 (high) on each qualification. On your form, too, there should be space at the bottom for comments, questions, missing information, and notes for committee discussion. Also at the bottom there should be a three-option, forced-choice overall rating: qualified, needs discussion, eliminate. Examples of these forms may be found at www.thesearchsource.org.

For the coaching, turn to your HR or career center director or perhaps a veteran administrator. All committee members—don't assume this knowledge—should be up to speed on how to read an administrative résumé.

For the actual reading, the chair should identify beforehand three quite different applications in the pool, each illustrating a key choice or two before the committee—a young but apparently brilliant applicant, an "overqualified" candidate from another sector, and a person with all the qualifications except a PhD, for example. Each member evaluates each application using the draft rating form, following which the ratings are compared and discussed: What accounts for our differences in rating? Why (or why not) would we bring this person forward? How do we feel about a JD instead of a PhD? and so on. In such discussion, the preferred qualifications are kept paramount; their use on actual applicants helps them come alive for members. The discussion that ensues—it deepens the ones started earlier and lays groundwork for decisions to come—is an important part of the unfolding conversation that lies at the heart of the committee's work.

At the end of this exercise, the committee reviews its experience with the draft rating form, makes any necessary adjustments, and adopts it for use with the full pool.

◆

A last step at this meeting is to decide how to prune your pool of inappropriate applications. No matter how careful your application procedure, your search for a provost will still generate submissions from graduate students, unhappy school superintendents, and dentists looking for second careers—people (and this is the criterion) the institution would never appoint.

Also in the pool you'll likely find some generic "applications" pumped out by websites. The chair, joined by a committee member or perhaps by your HR officer or search consultant, should be authorized to flag these candidacies in the files or on the website. This saves the full committee from a certain amount of fruitless reading and rating. Committee members can still look at these applications. If even one member thinks a flagged application should be discussed by the committee, there's no argument; put it back on the table.

The First Cut

At this point, let us say your 60-person pool has been pruned of inappropriate candidacies and is now at 50. Here you have a choice to make: should *every* committee member read *all* 50 files? Having everybody read everything has obvious advantages; the lean, three-part application you are using enhances chances for each member to read a larger number. The disadvantages are obvious in the use of valuable staff and faculty time. Most committees, especially with today's smaller pools, opt to have all members read all potentially viable files.

What if—this was more likely a decade or two ago—you have 150 total applications? With time pressing and committee members keeping busy schedules, an expedient must be devised. One is to split the pile, or divide it into three or four, and have two- or three-person teams do the reading. Another is to engage a consultant to "read down" the pile under your explicit instructions. (If you have engaged a search firm, it might perform this step for you.) A third is to ask the chair or a subcommittee to do all the reading and flag a next round of cuts, again, under full committee instruction and with the readers' unanimous agreement needed to eliminate any candidate. As before, any committee member can access all files and stipulate that a given candidacy should come before the full committee.

An important caution, as you review folders at early stages of screening—*watch your mindset*. "There are so many folders here, so much reading to do, we've *got* to cut these down. . . ." A "psychology of elimination" takes hold in which readers look for any excuse to get rid of someone ("Aha! Only a master's degree!"). It's at this point that mistakes are made, that the nontraditional or unusual candidacy is lost, that the pool gets stripped down to a midlevel common denominator. That mindset also may be why some women or minority candidates get lost.

The right mindset is that of *talent hunting*. As screeners you should be looking for interesting people who could bring something special to your position. A recommended procedure is for each committee-member reader, in the present example of cutting from 50 applications to perhaps a dozen, to bring forward a "find" who might not have scored well or written the perfect letter but who seems to bring something special to the search.

Screening for Talent

Let's turn to our 50 or so persons in the reduced pool and see how—with minimal bias and loss of talent—the committee might identify a dozen or so candidates for next levels of investigation. The step is tricky: with the obviously weaker applicants gone, chances for real mistakes rise.

The necessary thing at this stage is to establish a more systematic procedure for evaluating candidates, one that mines thoroughly the applicant information you have and keeps your eye on the specific position at stake. To these ends, the chair drafted and the committee approved a candidate-rating form. The quantification raised by this form will *not* prevent bias or decide any applicant's fate—only you can do that. A rating form helps *focus* individual reading and committeewide discussion.

With the form in hand, committee members (or subcommittees) read applicant files holistically against criteria of the preferred qualifications. All application parts are read together by each reader, following which the rating form is used to record judgments about candidate knowledge, skills, and abilities. (The application we recommend won't support "trait" rating.)

Experts provide additional tips for screening candidates at this stage. One is to do the rating as much as possible at one point in time; reading dribs and drabs of folders over busy days leads to impatient, inconsistent judgment. So set aside an afternoon and evening for your reading. A good practice at the start is to read several applications (including a mix of early and late submissions) before you begin rating individual candidates. Another tip is that your HR officer can show you how to sharpen the rating questions, resolve discrepant scores, improve inter-rater reliability, and use all numbers from one to five fully so the resulting spread is more marked (though too fine a point can be made of all this). Keep good notes of your ratings, comments, and judgments; you'll need these for committee-wide discussion. To safeguard confidentiality, do your reading in private.

As a matter of principle, committee members should excuse themselves from rating any candidate in whom they have a personal interest, and disclose that interest to the rest of the committee. A member who knows things about a candidate should share that knowledge with the committee and place a memo about it in the candidate's file. Internal candidates are an exception here: each might be rated by everyone, with each member's particular knowledge shared in discussion.

Review and Decision

With members' reading and rating of files now complete, it is time for them to reassemble as a committee, compare and discuss ratings, and select a small number of candidacies to go forward. A good tip is to schedule this meeting for a few days after the stated application date (not right on it); typically, a final wave of applications arrives just before or on that date and there is a delay in creating files and in members' reading of them. (Some of your best candidates—late recruits or fence-sitters—will apply at the very end.)

Most committees start this stage of screening by polling members, candidate by candidate, and posting their ratings on a chalkboard or newsprint. Some committees tally only final decisions (qualified, discuss,

THINKING ABOUT BIAS

Bias means specific things to a lawyer or a scientist; here it means any predisposition or act that stands between the committee and the fullest talent it can ultimately recommend. The two best guards against bias are thoughtful procedure and a good fix on the position and its preferred qualifications.

Words alone won't dispel the tenacity of academic discrimination on the basis of race or sex, religion or ethnic origin. You, of course, absolutely hope to avoid such bias. But committee after committee avows commitment to affirmative action, trumpets it in ads, finds a relevant candidate or two to keep alive for a while, then nominates a slate of white males. "We couldn't find a woman or Hispanic we liked," the refrain goes.

Part of the rueful committee's problem may have been an earlier failure to search actively for talented women and minorities. But just as often, it comes at the present stage, that of screening, in which pools that start with many such candidates are stripped dry at successive stages. This "stripping" occurs without apparent bias of race or sex, but occur it does, often on *non-job-related* grounds that reflect deeper biases or habits of mind.

One such bias operates in the reading of résumés. We're all eager to spot the "rising star," the "real comer"—Ivy grad, Phi Bete, a Rhodes, Berkeley PhD in physics or English, two books, a professorship, ready at 36 for your deanship. Whether you really *want* that "comer," who has his own agenda and may be your "goner" before he's 39, becomes moot; the profile is irresistible, whatever its (mis)match with your "preferred qualifications," which suddenly seem earnest and plodding.

Keep reminding yourself: The candidate profile you developed earlier does have meaning (and a lot of administration *is* earnest and plodding); the real talent you want for your position probably will *not* be "to the manor born." There are many good reasons why able people started out in colleges you never heard of, majored in nursing or sociology or teacher ed, display deviant "gaps" in their résumés (for community work, family, the army), took 13 years for a doctorate at a regional university, and are now working at a community college. Unless you're willing to look closely at what candidates have actually *achieved* and can *do* in your position, screening by "prestige" factors becomes a talent loser.

eliminate); others tally, too, the sum of all rating scores, in case the first tally eliminated someone who otherwise scored high—an oddity that may be good to identify and discuss. However the tally is done and the scores organized, it usually leads to a rough sorting of candidates into three categories: those who seem to have little or no committee support, those who most people seem to like, and a middle category of apparent lesser qualification or divided opinion.

Each of these categories is discussed in turn, starting with those candidates most people feel should be eliminated. This contradicts the natural tendency to start with the best, the top grouping, but discussing your people at the bottom, and *why* you put them there, sharpens committee wisdom about what it is really looking for. As you go through the individuals in that bottom group, all kinds of issues likely will surface: about academic pedigree, career stage, the weight attached to same-sector experience, and so on. It is important to surface at this stage, too, any added criteria or "hidden screens" individual members may have been using, such as recency of publications in candi-

Few screening factors seem stronger (and work to lose more talent) than bias by sector. It starts with negative inferences raised by baccalaureate origins. That "college I never heard of" turns out to be a women's college, or historically black, which the candidate attended for good reason and probably to good effect. "Why would we want somebody from a state college in Texas?" a screener snorts—and out goes a Hispanic candidate. "What's this person doing at Eastern Tech?" someone parries next—and an able woman gets the ax.

The great expansion of higher education since 1960, and the new mobility and social patterns emergent since then, render obsolete many of the familiar ways of judging academic careers. It's no longer possible to equate choice or need to work in a "second line" institution with "second rate" personal abilities. Factors of social commitment, tight job markets, geographic preference, and dual careers have "scattered talent all over the place," as one search consultant told us. "It's no problem for me to find a top Hispanic," he continued, "They're serving in community colleges, and these educators have a commitment. My problem is getting committees in four-year colleges to look at them."

Special blinders seem to apply across the divides of the public–private and two-year–four-year sectors, blinders regrettable for the inbreeding they prompt and for their negative effect on women and minorities. Search committees also tend too quickly to dismiss able candidates working for government (including state boards), foundations, professional associations, for-profit institutions, corporate universities, or who are working abroad.

"There are lots of talented, high-achieving women in academic administration today," an executive recruiter told us. "I find them in nursing schools, libraries, working as registrars or in extension programs, but you know what happens? They never make it beyond the second screening. My corporate clients are much better at this. They want a job done, they look at the abilities."

Our colleague Barbara Taylor of Academic Search has another take on search dynamics: "Most committees hope their institution will `marry up' with an appointment. But, understandably, most applicants are hoping to `marry up,' too. The upshot is that members obsess on a `top' fraction of the pool and overlook talent under their noses."

dates for a deanship. By talking these issues through, the committee fashions a better, collective sense of what a competitive candidate looks like—good preparation for discussing that more critical top group.

You are now ready to go to the top group. Here, again, these candidates should be discussed, one at a time. The fact that everyone rated them highly begs the reasons why. As you articulate those reasons, pay attention to shifting ideas about the relative importance of your various preferred qualifications and to the sources of unconscious bias in evaluating candidacies. Not uncommonly, two or three candidates, upon discussion, will fall out of the top group. (We've also seen "bottom-group" candidates, upon discussion, moved to the top.) All this underscores the point that it is the committee's deliberation and best judgment, not numeric ratings, that moves candidates forward.

After these two rounds of discussion, the committee is ready for its hardest task, that of deciding the fate of

WHAT IF YOUR CANDIDATE POOL IS SMALL?

This and prior chapters have assumed an applicant pool of several dozen, robust enough to bring three to four candidates to campus for interviews. What if, despite your very best efforts, you have only 18 applicants, just one or two of whom seem worth interviewing? Almost certainly, press ahead. Good people *are* hard to find, and the one you want may be in your pool, small as it is.

In these situations, we've seen committees throw up their hands in despair. But the days of 200-applicant pools may be gone forever. Committees, too, deceive themselves with rosy notions about the job's attractiveness.

What can also trip committees up in these situations is an original charge from the appointing officer to present "three appointable candidates," a time-honored formula sometimes too casually put to committees. In the circumstance that three cannot be found, the committee and appointing officer should weigh alternatives with a certain pragmatism. If all choose to proceed, it becomes even more important for the committee to carefully craft the interview, reference check, and courting process.

those in the middle. All of your prior deliberation—about eliminating and "gotta have" factors—comes into play here. Your apprehension now is about individuals your careful process may leave behind. Would your pool so far, if it were for the University of Chicago presidency in the 1920s, have included that 29-year-old law dean from afar, Robert Maynard Hutchins? Would your committee be open to a candidate for a senior communications position with no service in higher education but years of parallel experience at a major national corporation?

The way to proceed here is, as before, one candidate at a time on the basis of the preferred qualifications. There are few shortcuts; the ongoing criterion is that of apparent fitness to join the top group. This is a moment, too, to bring forward any "finds" that haven't been fully considered up to now. Depending on the size of the remaining top group, not uncommonly one to three candidates from the middle are moved up, joining the others in a semifinalist cohort.

How large should that cohort be? One answer is, no larger than the number of high-quality, potentially appointable people in your pool. Another answer is provided by what will come next: your calls to these candidates' references. This latter factor cuts two ways. You don't want so large a number (18, say) that you are presented with a nearly impossible list of calls to make

(upwards of a hundred). And you certainly don't want to subject to such calling any candidates (not to mention their references) that you are not confident you need to learn more about. Assuming a reasonably strong pool, the 50 applicants you are screening might typically be reduced to 8 to 12 candidates at this point, sometimes fewer, seldom more.

———◆———

The final task for the committee's screening meeting has to do with review and approval of an interview guide for the reference calls to come, and instruction on making the calls. The interview guide itself should be drafted ahead of time by the chair in consultation with your HR director, an experienced committee member, or perhaps a consultant. The point of the 8, 10, or 12 questions you'll pose to referents is to elicit information, as concrete and example filled as possible, about the candidate's knowledge, skills, abilities, and traits in relation to your preferred qualifications. If management abilities were among those qualifications, for example, a good question might ask a respondent to characterize the candidate's abilities along those lines, with probes about style, relationships with people, collaborative instincts, use of data, and habits of decision-making. A good interview pushes beyond the adjectives to learn of specific behaviors, instances, and outcomes. At www.thesearchsource.org, you'll find examples of interview guides from past searches and more detailed advice on the making of calls.

One special circumstance about calling deserves mention here: a committee with student members will recognize that students may not be in the best position to undertake telephone interviews with senior professionals from other colleges. There are two options, neither exclusive. One is to have them learn the art by sitting in on a few interviews done by senior committee members, perhaps taking the notes and discussing after the fact what was heard. The second is to ask students to troll the Web and see what they can turn up about candidates. Similarly, students or the committee's staff person might go to the library and run a Lexis/Nexis or other Internet search on your 8 to 12 people.

———◆———

At the end of your screening meeting, run your census again. Does your semifinalist pool include the number and quality of people you want? Are the numbers of women and persons of color adequate for your purposes? Above all, do your 8 to 12 people appear to include at least *several* potentially appointable people, candidates that you feel some excitement about? If not, this is the time to consider selective recruitment of missing strengths into your pool. You can rationalize a weak pool by saying, as committees do, "We're only looking for one!" but there are so many pitfalls and potential disappointments ahead that it would be most unwise to count on that one perfect candidate being there at the end. The best safeguard against a failed search is a robust pool with multiple competitive candidacies. So if your pool looks thin, stare that fact in the eye now and prepare to restart recruitment.

After the screening meeting, the chair usually takes the résumés of the 8 to 12 candidates the committee has chosen to the appointing officer for review and comment. If the officer deems the overall pool deficient (as you may have), again, it's best to know that now and move quickly to augment it. If the officer offers grounds

for not appointing a given candidate, the committee might want to drop that person now on the basis that there's no sense wasting time on a candidacy that will be a nonstarter. Remind the officer at this meeting that he or she is bound by committee pledges of confidentiality to candidates and that this is not a time for "off-list" phone calls to friends about candidates in the pool.

Assuming affirmation of the pool (even if recruitment may continue), the chair then calls the 8 to 12 remaining candidates to tell them of the committee's interest and of their advancement in the search, asks about further questions or information needs, and conveys what will come next (calls to their named references *only*). The chair wants two outcomes from these calls to candidates: the candidates' continuance in the search and a green light to contact their references. On the latter score, some candidates may ask that you wait a day or two while they alert references to the coming calls; of course, honor that request. A candidate unwilling to have you make calls at this point probably needs to be put on hold or dropped, and be told so.

The chair should also have looked closely at the list of five provided references. Does it include people on the candidate's home campus with direct knowledge of his or her work? That's what you want, indeed need. But some submitted lists will be filled out with distant endorsers and character references. If so, now is the time to get the names, numbers, and permission to call people truly familiar with the candidate's recent work.

Two Busy Weeks

For committee members, the next two weeks will be among the most demanding of all. Each member is likely to have five to ten reference calls to complete—no small task, given busy professional schedules. The people you are calling are probably as busy as you are; the grief of telephone tag can be alleviated by making phone appointments with your respondents. The search assistant might make some of these appointments for you, and offer to e-mail your prospectus to informants so they'll understand your search and position better. To reduce bias and get consistent information across candidates, all callers should use the

---

BETTER INFORMATION FROM INFORMANTS

In a recent *Chronicle of Higher Education* column, Clara Lovett, the former president of AAHE and former president of Northern Arizona University, speaks for many of the senior people you'll call in her list of the turn-off behaviors she encounters from committees checking references:

- ◆ Failure to provide her in advance with useful information about the campus and the position, so there is no basis for thought beforehand or for making judgments about "fit"
- ◆ Hasty, rushed interview calls placed by a person who clearly has a script to get through and more important matters to return to
- ◆ Longer and longer lists of canned questions—which may crowd out what the reference-giver really thinks
- ◆ Recommendations sought by e-mail
- ◆ An undertone of arrogance, a sense that the search committee is doing the candidate a favor by talking with you

---

committee's approved interview guide. These typically have 8 to 12 questions (with probes) built around your preferred qualifications; again, examples are located on www.thesearchsource.org.

Most committee members will have done these calls before and know there's an art to reference checking. The people you're calling may be distracted, suspicious, or protective. Your need is to convince them that you're a bona fide caller with an organized, professional purpose, that you have a sincere interest in the candidate, and that their report matters. Explain your purpose, take time to chat and establish rapport, ask credible questions, and be a good listener. Don't interrupt or rush on; leave time for volunteered remarks. Probe as necessary to get beyond strings of adjectives to specific incidents and how they were handled: reports of critical events add depth and concreteness to the larger picture you are trying to build. A good interviewer doesn't waste time asking respondents about what you both already know—that the candidate has experience with collective bargaining, for example. Ask instead how the candidate behaves at the bargaining table and to what effect. Yes, the candidate is a good fund-raiser; how does he or she go about it? What were the results? At the end of an interview ask who are the two or three

people who know the candidate's work best. Save those names for later.

Note that search-committee members cannot ask informants questions about a candidate that it would be illegal to ask a candidate directly. Prohibited questions can vary by state and institutional policy but they typically proscribe asking, even indirectly, about a candidate's age, race, color, disability, marital status, nationality, ethnic origin, and the like. Keep your questions job related. Note that these same strictures will apply to all subsequent reference calls and interviews, on campus and off.

———◆———

In the course of reviewing candidate materials and talking with references, committee members often identify pieces of missing information or a point they want to know more about—like an unexplained midyear departure from a job. Any items of this kind should be collected by the chair and put to candidates with a request for response before the committee meets again.

Committees at this point can also ask candidates to add a brief work sample or two to their application: a decision memo, article, or program evaluation,

MORE ON CALLING REFERENCES

For a search committee, the frequent bane of reference checks is inconsistent information: Too many members are making the calls, asking different questions, recording responses in various ways, and so on, so that it is difficult back in committee to have well-founded information that allows comparative evaluation of candidates, which is the task. Here are strategies committees have used to overcome this hurdle:

Use an interview guide. This ensures that important, core matters are covered with respondents and provides for a more consistent, easy-to-use recording of responses. The best interviewers always use such a guide, but in a free, conversational way, so that the respondent never has a sense of simply being led through obligatory questions.

Paired interviews. You might have two committee members conduct all reference calls or at least the most important ones, perhaps with one person doing the questions and another recording answers, then both agreeing at the end on the accuracy of the resulting record. The intent of the procedure is to reduce bias in the recording of responses and achieve a fuller record of the call. The drawbacks are that it can be difficult to arrange three-person conversations, and the procedure multiplies the sheer amount of committee time devoted to the task. With two members on the line, too, it can be harder to establish the easy, trusting relationship with an informant that promotes candor.

Single caller. Another option is to have one person do all or most of the calling. This presumes the availability of an experienced person with the time, knack, and confidence of the committee. The reward can be better overall questioning, consistency of information across candidates, and a great saving in committee-member time. But the method puts high reliance on a single reporter, and other committee members wind up with little personal feel for their candidates.

Divvy up the calls. A modest but useful guard against bias is to assign calls about each candidate to different committee members. This avoids the trap of a single committee member calling a string of one candidate's references, falling in love with that candidate on the first call, then starting to hear in subsequent calls only what confirms that positive impression. The committee member winds up back in your meeting, not as the reporter or analyst you want, but as an advocate.

---

for example, or an office annual report authored by the candidate. A few candidates—this practice will be common soon—will have an "administrative portfolio" to share electronically with the committee. By all means welcome such portfolios: the best will be but 10 to 12 pages long and will provide you with a good window into job-related knowledge and abilities in use. As such pieces arrive, put them in the files or on your website or portal for committee reading.

Finally, a smart step at this point is for the chair to remind candidates that the neutral-site (or telephone) interviews will occur on dates X and Y, and to save time then for a potential conversation with the committee. (You've already sent these people a search schedule, but they'll appreciate the reminder.)

If you began candidate review with 60 applicants, now may be the time to send the 50 or so that you set aside a letter of respect and gratitude informing them that they are no longer under consideration. (Check with your HR office; it may have a policy on this.)

Identifying Candidates for Interview

After two busy weeks of calling and conferring, the search committee is again ready to convene, this time to identify the candidates it wishes to speak with face-to-face. All the work of the past days will now come to the table: your talks with references, new materials from candidates, and the results of your Web searching. The task is to identify, from among the 8 to 12 you've been investigating, the smaller number—perhaps 5 to 8—you'll invite to interview. You'll identify those people through sustained discussion, candidate by candidate, in full committee. Set aside appropriate time in a comfortable room for the task: given all the reports you need to hear about each candidate, it can take a full afternoon. The chair's leadership skills and the committee's sense of mutual regard count a lot at this juncture.

It's hard to advise a group on just how to proceed through such a crucial session, other than to be mindful of what's already been said in this *Handbook*: mine carefully the information you have, stay focused on the job qualifications as you defined them, ask who fits them and would perform best, and be mindful of your own biases. Some committees, after all the reports on a candidate have been heard, ask each member to rate him or her on the form used earlier, to keep eyes on the stated qualifications. One rule most committees insist upon: in selecting finalists, no single individual can block or insist upon a given candidacy. Candidates move forward by consensus, achieved through group discussion.

Selecting "five to eight" finalists is arbitrary but has good reasons. If you will conduct neutral-site interviews and are limited to two days, eight will be about the maximum number of people you can meet with; if

one day, four or five will be the most you can see. If these interviews constitute your final screen before bringing two to four to campus, you may want to see twice that number to be confident about those you invite, given the possibility of withdrawals and the likelihood that some of your choices will not show well in interviews.

Our advice is *not* to start with a number in your head: "We have eight slots to fill, let's tally the forms and be done with it." What you want to do is figure out how many motivated, appointable candidates—people you actually feel some enthusiasm for—you have in your pool. A robust pool may have eight, a thinner one just three.

———◆———

Once the committee has identified the people it wants to meet with, thought about the intended interviewing is in order. Our steps so far have assumed that five to eight candidates may be brought to a neutral site—a nearby airport hotel, perhaps, away from campus scrutiny to safeguard confidentiality—for formal interview. This procedure takes a big chunk of committee time, of course, and may well incur travel costs of $5,000 to $10,000. For positions at the deanship level and above, the effort and expense are more than justified.

For director and associate-level positions, and where budgets pinch, committees often opt for a more economical step, that of interviewing candidates by telephone; modern audioconferencing equipment has made such interviews easier and more natural. Video and Internet-based interviews have also become a possibility, though some colleges and candidates still find them difficult to arrange. Search veterans argue that you can learn more from face-to-face interaction than from any electronic hook-up, but they agree, too, that telephone interviews can be helpful in moving beyond paper to a fuller sense of a person. Audioconferences have their own sources of bias—some candidates will be more comfortable talking over the phone, or just sound better—so no committee should overinterpret what it hears.

———◆———

After you've identified the five to eight people you wish to speak with, three steps of communication lie ahead:

First, the chair should call the successful candidates, express happiness about that outcome, describe the intended interviews, ask again if there are questions, and note that a packet of fuller information will be in the mail. You made a plan for mailings like this in chapter 2; a packet at this stage might include the institution's strategic plan, an accreditation report, budget information, the campus fact book, documents related to the position, an organizational chart, information on fringe benefits, and brochures about the local area and housing. Tell these candidates, too, how to schedule a specific date and time to speak with the committee. (The search secretary can coordinate the scheduling here.)

A second round of calls should then be made to the candidates just eliminated to tell them of that fact. Since they know your schedule, they'll appreciate your calling right away. A special circumstance is the candidate or two who may have been "put on hold." The best advice is not to temporize but to tell them of that status right away. Not infrequently, the person on hold will withdraw. But an especially motivated person may hang in there with you.

A final step of communication recognizes that the committee's work over the past weeks has no doubt been watched with interest across campus. While the committee deliberates, a "second conversation" whirls outside its chambers, compounded of rumor, hope, and apprehension about the process. The committee's pledge to itself of "no leaks, no private reporting" is never more important than now. This is a good moment, then, for a progress report to the campus from the chair.

Summing Up

In this chapter, an applicant pool of 60 was reduced to an interview group of 5 to 8. The trick in screening is to winnow down an applicant pool to a manageable number of candidates without losing the best talent you worked to build into that pool.

For the winnowing, this chapter recommends taking things in steps—culling out first the most inappropriate applications, then proceeding at successive stages with greater formality and care, and at a key stage obtaining new information from candidates—as you advance toward a finalist group.

As guards against talent loss, reminders about bias, a "census," and "add-backs" were recommended. These reinforce the point made in chapter 4 that the idea of a search committee is to *search* for talent.

EQUAL TREATMENT?

Through the stages of screening described in this chapter, should any candidates receive "preferential treatment?"

The universal advice of committee veterans is "no." The reason is fairness, as much to yourself and the search's integrity as to candidates. Let the talent rise to the top. As for being sure that "certain candidacies" are treated "fully and well," the safest course is to treat all candidacies that way.

Are there exceptions to this rule? As mentioned earlier, there may be internal circumstances that make it wise for a committee to bring forward to the interview stage an admired internal candidate or an "acting." By the same token, it may be fairest to such a colleague and to the search *not* to bring to interview a person with no realistic chance of appointment, especially when that interview slot could be used to meet with one more candidate who *is* appointable.

What about people you've specially recruited? These should come into the pool on the same basis as everyone else, indeed without labels that they were someone's recruits. If something special is known about them that prompted the recruitment, share that with the full committee. But no good case can be made for stringing along a candidacy that just isn't competitive. The same goes for that "special" candidate nominated by your president or an influential legislator.

Committees have been known to keep alive candidacies of women or minorities just because of their status. But how sensible or fair can that be when the object of screening is to bring forward people with real potential to be appointed? If you no longer have appointable minority or women candidates at this stage, the right step is to stop and renew your recruitment.

In higher-level searches, there may be people at this stage that you do not enter into the screening process at all. These are your "prospects," that small number of talented people you are still trying to interest in the job and who are not yet formal applicants.

CHAPTER 6

The Interviews:
Knowing and Courting Candidates

This longest of the Handbook's *chapters will help your search committee work through an important set of next questions: how to interview your remaining candidates, how many to bring to campus, how to structure those visits for mutual learning, and how to complete your evaluation of the finalists. By chapter's end, the committee should have gathered all the information it needs to proceed with recommendations to the appointing officer.*

Initial Interviews

In the last chapter, we reduced our mythical pool to a manageable five to eight finalists. Now it's time for the committee as a whole to speak directly with these candidates.

As we indicated in the last chapter, there are two options for how to proceed. For a high-level search (provost, vice president, some deanships), we recommend that if at all possible you conduct in-person, neutral-site interviews. For director and associate-level positions and when budgets are an issue, committees can interview candidates by phone or videoconference. Whichever fits your situation, both interview formats have the following features:

- A carefully crafted interview guide drawn directly from the preferred qualifications
- An interview that is long enough (we recommend an hour and a half) for fuller interaction between the candidate and committee
- A thoughtful debriefing by the committee after each interview

Neutral-site interviews are usually held off campus, away from prying eyes, in the interests of maintaining confidential participation in your search. A good location is at a hotel with easy shuttle access from a major airport. This may require committee travel to a larger city, but the advantages of a big-city airport in protecting anonymity and avoiding the uncertainties of connecting flights are worth it. You want to rent two rooms: a large conference room with an interview-friendly square table in it, and a second, smaller room for candidate greeting and waiting. You'll need your committee's staff assistant with you to welcome candidates and usher them in and out of the room in ways that prevent them from running into one another. The assistant also provides candidates with an expense form for travel reimbursement. Refreshment setups should be available in both rooms. A nifty idea for warming up a sterile interview room is to bring along a large picture display of your campus—the type your admissions staff uses at college nights.

As for interviewing by phone, our one tip is to use, if at all possible, modern audioconferencing equipment, which produces superior voice quality, avoids clipped conversations, and suppresses background noise.

For these interviews, you'll need a set of prepared questions. The chair can draft these beforehand and e-mail them to the committee for review. Your dozen or so questions will be drawn directly from the preferred qualifications and include probes and follow-up questions. Not infrequently, committee members will find ways to choose a question, customize it, and make a line of questioning their own. All committee members should feel free to interpose a follow-up question in the spirit of keeping things conversational between the group and the candidate (but don't turn this into a grilling). Again, all questions should be as behavior and performance oriented as possible—you are looking for specific instances and accomplishments—and, of course, they must be legally permissible.

Examples of interview guides used in prior searches are posted at www.thesearchsource.org. On that website, too, you'll find further hints about how to make neutral-site interviews go more smoothly.

Interviews of an hour and a half are recommended. This allows for time to greet and chat with candidates at the start and end, for an hour of committee members' questions, plus time for the candidate's questions. You need a half-hour break between interviews to debrief one interview and prepare for the next, with an allowance for restroom breaks and phone calls. Add up the time and you'll see why committees are wise to schedule no more than four interviews a day.

———— ◆ ————

Before each interview, the committee would do well to remind itself of what has been learned about the candidate through the application, references, and other sources. Note any outstanding questions you have about the person (the "wish we knews" identified earlier); these can now be put to the interviewee. The committee should also remind itself that the tone of the interviews should be welcoming and conversational, that these sessions have dual objectives of learning and courting.

Candidates with experience in these kinds of interviews know reasonably well what to expect and, indeed, what to say—all will aver that they are "collaborative" and a "good listener." So you don't look to these interviews to help you decide whether a candidate is a good manager, for example. You learn how candidates manage and get work done by talking with people on their home campuses. What you can learn in an interview is how they think about themselves as managers and what they believe their values and accomplishments might be.

These interviews also become an occasion for probing the substance and depth of a candidate's thinking about issues of the position. What does your potential dean of arts and sciences, for example, think about general education or the Boyer/Rice version of faculty evaluation or the AAUP statement on shared governance? What has he or she done to enact those views? Is there real depth and thoughtfulness behind them? Does the candidate display awareness of larger developments nationally? knowledge of situations on your own campus as described in the materials sent or on your website?

Keep in mind the pitfalls of these interviews, too:

- Research on interviewing shows that committee members subconsciously make up their minds about a candidate in the initial minutes of the meeting—based on the person's gender and race, height and dress, manner of greeting, opening words, and so on—then for the remainder of the interview tend to hear what confirms this impression. All of us, too, tend to exaggerate our abilities to "know it when we see it" and therefore to overvalue what we can learn from these brief, contrived encounters.

- Committees often fall in love with the first available candidate. That is, the committee has worked so patiently up to now with abstract, once-removed information (résumés, reference notes, etc.) that the presence at last of a real candidate—attractive, articulate, interested in our job(!)—tends to make it forget all of its stated criteria, earlier information, and other candidates in favor of this marvelous "bird in hand."

- Candidates are quite aware that they confront a test and are on stage. People good at the process know how to present themselves, parry questions, hold the initiative, even fool you. Some people show well in interviews, others don't; often there's little correlation between interview performance and job performance.

How to combat these tendencies? Self-reminders and gadfly remarks can help; so will careful listening, staying focused on your preferred qualifications, and keeping the results of reference checking before you.

After each interview, committees should conduct a ten-minute debriefing. What did we hear? Were the candidate's responses notably strong or weak, reassuring or troubling on any front? What impressions did we form about the person's ability to succeed in our environment? Committee members should then use time during the break to make notes for themselves about the candidate for later discussion and decision making at the conclusion of all interviews, especially noting this candidate's strengths or weaknesses in relation to the preferred qualifications.

Committees should also ask themselves, how did *we* do? Could any aspect of our welcome or interaction with candidates be improved? Consciously or not, committees can in turn seem disorganized, sleepy-headed, inquisitorial, or just plain discourteous. (We have seen a good candidate leave a "successful" interview and withdraw from a search.) In these interviews, candidates are making up their minds about the institution and the search, and the committee is the personification of both.

Deciding Whom to Bring to Campus

At the end of all phone or neutral-site interviews (tired as you may be!), the committee needs to remain in place and come to judgment on the candidates just interviewed. What, indeed, do we now know about them? Keep all references and interview notes, other information that may have been adduced, and your preferred qualifications before you as you proceed through the roster a candidate at a time. It may prove easy to eliminate one or two persons, and a couple of other candidates may have evoked genuine enthusiasm. The difficulty, of course, lies with those in between.

The parameters here are set by the number of people you intend to invite to campus and present to col-

leagues in the next step of the process. How many people should that be? The most important, even determining, factor ought to be the number of true standouts in your pool. You simply don't want to waste your and other people's time with dull, risky, or underprepared aspirants.

Committees usually begin with the "rule of three," that three is an optimal number to bring to campus, given that you want comparative perspective on your best candidates and to control the expense and time of visits. When five or seven are brought to campus, for example, the strain of arrangement making on everybody's time becomes palpable. Bringing five to seven to campus can also be a sign of overvaluing such exposure. Eighty percent of what you need to know about candidates should come from determined reference checking and quiet homework, not public Q&A sessions.

Two other factors may be in play at this juncture. One is that institutional bylaws for search (if they exist) or the committee's charge may already state the number to be brought to campus. The other is that the charge may specify that the appointing officer wants the committee to present for potential appointment three candidates the committee believes are qualified. In that case, you surely want to bring four to campus, knowing that at least one may prove unacceptable or drop out. Some committees opt for a fourth candidate in any case, choosing for that slot a less traditional but potentially high-gain choice. But again, if there are just two candidates who genuinely stand out (and your charge and bylaws permit), invite just those two to campus.

When the committee has settled on the identity of those it will invite, a number of tasks remain. The committee should review its own, the appointing officer's, and institutional calendars to confirm best days for the scheduling of campus visits. Preferences for the length and conduct of visits should be discussed. Pending candidate continuance and approval, make plans now for a new set of "off list" reference calls.

At meeting's end, the chair should telephone the candidates the committee has decided to bring to campus; let them know right away of the committee's high regard and invitation to go forward in the search. The successful candidates should also be briefed on what will come next: a call from the committee's staff assistant to arrange a campus visit, then a set of off-list reference calls to colleagues on the candidate's present and former campuses. (The timing and any limitations on calling should be discussed with the candidate now.) Within a day or two, the unsuccessful candidates should receive a call conveying the outcome and expressing the committee's gratitude and professional regard. The appointing officer should be briefed on the outcome. And the campus at large should receive an e-mail telling of the committee's delight at identifying finalists and of the opportunity they'll have soon to meet with candidates and provide feedback. To safeguard confidentiality as long as possible, and if campus regulations so permit, candidate names and vitas may be posted one at a time just before each visit.

It is also conceivable at this point that the search itself could be put on hold because the finalist group just doesn't seem sufficiently capable or diverse. In this circumstance, the committee may want to loop back into its semifinalist pool to identify two or three additional candidates for intensive investigation, or court anew one of its "prospects," or reopen the search to recruit two or three newcomers to the final group. Each of these steps represents a shift in course and calls for the committee chair to confer with the appointing officer.

After the chair's call to the successful candidates, the scheduling of visits is done by the search committee's staff assistant. This entails finding a day or two for the visit itself, help with travel arrangements, and lining up campus officials and groups to meet with each candidate.

Deep Background Checks

At this stage, with perhaps three candidates in the running, the work of the committee takes a subtle shift. The need now is more explicitly *twofold*: to know these three "better than their mothers do," as one search veteran advises, *and* to court them. The object is to find the person who best fits the job as you've described it, and to do so in a way that disposes him or her to respond favorably to a subsequent institutional offer.

This knowing-courting process can be tricky. A committee can be detective-like in its inquiries and drive a candidate away, or it can so defer to a candidate's reluctance that it learns too little.

Some or all of your candidates are likely to be in sensitive positions. Up to now, everything has gone forward quietly, even your calls to the candidates' named references (who tend to be trusted friends), so little has been at risk. Now, by letting you make unrestricted calls to the home campus and by traveling for a public interview, each candidate risks exposure and scrutiny, and for what? One chance in three? At least two in your group won't be hired, as each knows; none wants to jeopardize or be undercut in an existing position.

To show your professional regard for their situations, the chair should consult with each candidate about whom on their home campus may now be called. (On some campuses, candidates complete and fax back a permission form for these calls.) From your standpoint, of course, you'd like a green light to contact anybody with potential knowledge of the candidate's abilities. A committee that has done the right things until now—provided good information aimed at motivating candidates, kept in touch, communicated personal caring, and been professional about its work—has a better chance of enjoying candidate confidence and getting that green light.

Often, and for good reason, a candidate has to ask for limits: a sitting academic dean, for example, may be seriously undercut if committee members suddenly rain long-distance phone calls on randomly chosen faculty and staff back home; a formal reference call to his or her president may also be inappropriate at this stage, as might be one to a union head who is pursuing a grievance to which the dean is party. Even so, at this stage that dean must allow your committee reasonable access to people familiar with his or her work, or withdraw.

Assuming full permission, search professionals at this stage like to complete as many as a dozen additional off-list phone calls about each candidate (or enough for a full picture to emerge). Your committee has already called five or so named references provided by the candidate; study notes from these calls for clues about what you seem to know already and for lines of questioning you'll pursue next. Search professionals do not discount reports from named references but regard them as only a start: they'll call people they *think* should know the candidate, then the candidate's supervisor, staff, colleagues, and secretary, then do a blitz of former institutions, *then* pursue extra leads or a hunch.

Along the way, knowing that an active administrator cannot please everybody, executive recruiters aren't put off by any one person's "negative" comments; the search is for *patterns* of strength and limitation, for indications of "fit" between a person and your task. Nor is every remark accorded equal weight: the inquirer evaluates "where the respondent is coming from," how credible and candid a source it is, how recently and well the respondent knew the candidate, and so on, all in the interests of a fair picture.

We discussed how to conduct reference calls in chapter 5, so if necessary, review that information before you begin making calls. Here are reminders and a tip:

- Use an interview guide that has been created and approved by the committee. The guide at this stage, reflecting what you already know, may be shorter and contain leading questions to prompt freer, less predictable responses. (What kind of a person and professional is the candidate? What have been the candidate's major accomplishments? disappointments? If I walked your campus and talked with other people, what different reactions to the candidate would I encounter?)
- While one or two committee members, working in tandem, may do most of the calling about a given candidate, all other committee members should place a call to their own counterparts (e.g., chair of sociology, director of summer sessions) at the candidate's most recent institutions. Peer-to-peer conversations often bring high-candor reports.

Campus Visits: The Context

In thinking through this next, crucial phase of its work, the committee might ponder what it now knows and doesn't know about its candidates, so that objectives may be laid for the visits.

By now, for example, the committee should have a quite strong sense that each of the candidates has the knowledge and abilities to do the job as described, and a good sense of *how* each of them performs relevant work. You got this primarily from your reference calls, basing your judgments chiefly on an analysis of candidates' recent performance on tasks relevant to your job. As we said before, your answers to these questions should constitute a good 80 percent of what you'll base your final recommendations on.

Conversely, there's a residue of items that you have less information about. Until you talk in depth with the candidate, and until he or she has had a chance to look at your position up close, it's hard to know whether that position truly will motivate the candidate and whether he or she will want to do the job as you've defined it.

As yet, you have only a spotty sense of the candidates' specific views on substantive issues relevant to the position. (What does your candidate vice president for administration feel about outsourcing, for example?) And finally, having seen these people only briefly or interviewed them by phone, you're still not sure about factors like candidate–institution "chemistry," about the candidates' personal traits, matters of style, and acceptability to your colleagues—in short, whether the "match" or "fit" is such that the person will be effective in your institution.

The other side of the coin is that the candidates themselves have questions, both general (What do these people want? Would this be a good move for me? What are the risks here?) and quite specific (What's the office budget like? What quality of staff will I inherit? What's it like to work with this president or vice president?) Candidates, in short, are asking, "Do I want this job?"

Campus visits, then, inherently have a dual purpose: to promote two-way learning and two-way attraction—matchmaking, if you will.

———————◆———————

Each visit should be planned with the needs of the candidate in mind. To conserve visit time, ask the candidate by phone what final dose of information about the locale, institution, and position might be sent ahead of time (e.g., a three-year budget, information on local schools). Ask if a travel advance would be helpful, about meal and housing preferences (use a hotel, not a committee member's home), about questions they hope to have answered on the visit and people they'd like to see.

For senior positions, a two-day visit is almost always indicated, for the sake of your own needs and so that the candidate isn't confronted with a blizzard of rushed interviews and appointments with nary a chance to breathe, walk around, or think. Candidates will differ in their preferences or needs for scheduling; you show regard by consulting with each in advance about best arrangements for his or her travel and time on campus. Monday evening through Wednesday lunch, for example, may fit best with office, home, and airline schedules.

When the candidate is on campus have a committee member on hand for transitions between appointments, to attend to creature comforts, to answer questions and give feedback, to brief groups in advance and provide introductions, and to collect feedback forms.

Planning the Visits

The committee's task now is to plan the best use of on-campus time so that it learns as much as possible about its candidates. The matter is often overlooked. "We've done these before, it's all common sense," someone will say. Unfortunately, what too often happens is that finalists are endlessly whisked around past every conceivable person and group; they get worn out and turned off. On campus, snap judgments fly around

and feedback from interviewers is spotty at best, so the committee regroups afterwards with no good idea of what was learned from it all.

Given these pitfalls, it is helpful to line up your objectives, allocate time, and set up a plan to realize them. One such plan might have the following elements:

1. To provide each candidate with a fair picture of the campus setting and role and to enhance interest in the position, information giving and question answering should be planned as a first order of business.
2. To ascertain the candidate's views on important issues of substance—philosophy, approach, or personal agenda———the committee and other parties should conduct structured interviews around the most important of these topics.
3. To get a feel for "fit" and acceptability, and to let the candidate learn about key people and constituencies he or she may be working with, serial interviews with a range of campus parties should be arranged.
4. To get a further reading on how candidates would perform relevant tasks in your setting, the committee might arrange situations in which each performs a task or two in public and is thereby judged.
5. To get a sense of compatibility and attraction between the candidate and appointing officer (this will be important to both of them), time should be set aside for extended conversation between the two.

———————◆———————

Placing these objectives alongside what's just been said in these pages about interviewing, we now detail how each of them—the building blocks for the schedule you arrange—might be realized.

The Finalist's Questions
In a spirit of using the visit to enhance interest in the position, a first objective is to see that the candidate's issues and concerns surface and are addressed, *and* that

the person learns fully your sense of the position and the opportunity you believe it presents.

Some of a candidate's questions can be dealt with more economically by the chair and the candidate alone, beforehand on the phone or on the way in from an airport. But a good idea for a first meeting between the candidate and full committee is to devote most of that up-front time to the *candidate's* questions. The message you thereby send is one of considerate regard. But your own interests can also be served by this step: through it you can learn, early in the visit while there's still time to do something about them, what issues are at stake in the visit from the finalist's point of view.

Your committee can learn more than a little, too, simply by listening to the questions candidates ask. Are they prepared? Skeptical? Incisive? Did your would-be librarian ask only about the benefits package? Did your would-be comptroller evince no interest in seeing the institution's long-form audit? The committee might well stay behind after this session and ask, What questions did we hear? What do they tell us?

Other parts of the two days will be used to enhance candidate knowledge of the locale, institution, and position. A drive around town, a walking tour of the campus, time to visit with people who work in the office of the position, plus appointments with administrative peers, the appointing officer, and president would follow in due course. On many campuses, it's the practice in group interviews to reserve the final 15 to 20 minutes for questions asked by the candidate. The search committee's final meeting with the candidate might end that same way.

The goal behind all these steps is clear: you want each candidate to leave with a full sense of your personal regard, of having had his or her questions answered, and of knowing fully the opportunities in your position. The bottom line is that you are trying to *recruit* a candidate's active interest; let that fact supersede any other. Unless and until the candidate wants the job, all the evaluation you do is irrelevant.

Candidate Views

In collegiate search, much more so than in corporate search (where this point tends to be passed over lightly), it can be important to learn the specific views of candidates on issues of substance. Ideas matter on a campus; you'd expect heads of major offices to come with a point of view if not a specific agenda, and you'll therefore organize interview time to learn about those views and agendas.

Here at last comes an appropriate task for the much-maligned (but inevitable) large-group interviews you'll schedule. These *can* work to elucidate candidate views, *if* they are so oriented and prepared for.

The search chair should meet ahead of time with interview groups to pose the questions, What are we trying to find out here? What job-related things do we hope to know about this candidate when this group's interview is concluded? For example, a dozen or more faculty members will interview candidates as a group for an academic deanship, and you (and they) want to know the candidate's approach to general education. Ask one member of that group to pose the question directly: "What is your philosophy of general education? What do you think students should be able to know and do when they graduate?" That questioner stays in charge of the discussion for ten minutes or more, upon which a second might take over with a more specific, angled approach: "Some faculty members believe we should go back to a great books approach; what are the pros and cons of that in your view?" Ask a third interviewer later still to try something even more particular to your campus about value-added assessment, or problem-based learning, or science for nonmajors, for example.

The point is that, with just a bit of rehearsal and planning, this group's interview can produce an assessment of real depth of the candidate's approach to undergraduate education.

It makes sense, too, to think ahead about group composition in relation to questions you want answered. In a visit by a candidate for head librarian, for example, it's easy to imagine appropriate sets of questions that might be posed by successive interview groups of students, faculty members, library professionals, and the senate's library committee. The key to getting the knowledge you want lies in your own planning, coaching of interviewers, and provisions for feedback. (A side benefit of your coaching is that it helps interviewers understand their role and its context within a larger, thoughtful process.)

A caution in all this is that no search committee would presume to know all the substantive issues at stake in a given vacancy. Therefore, don't over-prescribe for your interviewers; be ready to learn from their initiative. Nor should any interview look staged or aim to put a candidate on the spot.

The committee's goal at the end of two days is to know what each candidate stands for and would likely bring as an agenda. Its question at that point becomes, How does the candidate's agenda match our own sense of what the institution and position require?

Candidate Fit

Questions of "fit" are equally on your mind and the candidate's. Your basic question is this: Does the candidate's background and personal style augur well for successful functioning on our campus?

In collegiate institutions, style and affect do matter for administrative effectiveness. In various institutions, administrators tend to be person-oriented academics or task-oriented workaholics, "tweedy" or "down home," gregarious, managerial, religious, or outdoorsy. Each college, too, has its distinctive faculty and student cultures, mediated by governance structures. The committee's goal is to find a person *reasonably* congruent with these cultures and who can work effectively within them.

The committee can expect lots of feedback about "fit," "style," and "chemistry" from campus interviewers. Often this will come through in the form of varying levels of *liking* for candidates. (That's what people make up their minds about in the initial minutes of an interview.) Listen, of course, to what any campus interviewer has to say about the attractiveness of any candidate, but keep a grain of salt handy. You're not running a beauty contest; charm alone won't get a job done. That focus—on getting a job done—is one for the committee to stay attuned to even as others fall in love with this or that candidate. In fact, you are not looking for the "most liked" candidate; you are looking for abilities matched to a position. But you also know that to succeed in the job, a candidate must at least win the respect of relevant constituencies.

The same thinking applies to the larger question of fit. The issue is not, Who is most like us? That's a recipe

for losing talent, and especially female, minority, and nontraditional candidacies. Indeed, the thing some campuses need is the fresh air and difference just such a candidate would bring. Again, the "fit" you seek is a person sufficiently in tune with your culture to work effectively in it.

There is still another aspect of "fit" that will come into play in a campus visit, namely the congruence between a candidate's views and values and the mission of the institution. This will be most at issue with upper-level appointments. In a search for a new vice president or dean, then, it would be a good idea to ask the other vice presidents or deans to probe the matter. If these groups work as a team, they will also look at candidates for wisdom and complementarity.

Indeed, some of the shrewdest judgments about candidates, the committee will find, will come from administrators in parallel positions or who report to the same appointing officer. It's therefore a good idea for a committee searching for a division chair, for example, to schedule candidate interviews with other division chairs; they know the job and what it takes. Similarly, it is always a good idea to schedule candidate time with direct reports and people in the office the candidate would head; they know best its culture and work requirements and have no small stake in the outcome.

◆

As noted at the outset, the question of "fit" is two-sided, the other of which is the fit for the candidate. He or she undoubtedly will want to get a sense in the visit of the people and resources the position entails working with: What will my colleagues here be like? Are they able, loyal, and welcoming? What are people expecting of me? Can I work with the appointing officer? Will that officer stay or leave? Have I gotten a full and true picture of the financial situation of the place? the vicissitudes of working in its culture? A good candidate will be forthcoming about these matters, which can be honored by the committee in the schedule it lays out and by allocating time for the candidate's questions.

A final observation about fit: In executive search, corporate recruiters emphasize to candidates at the visit

THE CANDIDATE'S MAKEUP

Even as it learns more about each candidate's relevant knowledge and abilities, a search committee might keep in mind that it knows little yet about his or her professional motivations, preferred work style, emotional predispositions, and so on—all of which bear on the questions, Will this job prompt best effort from this candidate along lines we want? Is there the right mix of challenge, people, and situation here to engage this person's best energies?

Executive searches in corporations, NGOs, and government attempt to answer these questions in two ways. One is through an extended, focused interview with the candidate, often lasting three to five hours. In such an interview, many details of family history, schooling, situations from prior employment, leisure and reading patterns, and the like are evoked, from which key aspects of the person's makeup are inferred. In the course of a longer, professionally done interview with a candidate, it's possible to get a firsthand sense of important "intangibles" like self-concept, achievement-motivation, reaction to stress and criticism, risk-taking, sense of realism about shortcomings, attention to detail, ethical orientation, and dispositions to lead.

A second way of getting at many of these variables—this is sometimes done in conjunction with the interview—is through a test of executive orientation (like the Princeton-based Caliper Profile or instruments from the Center for Creative Leadership). These tests attempt to predict executive performance along multiple dimensions; they take an hour or two to complete, may be done onsite or online, cost a few hundred dollars, and result in next-day written and oral feedback to the committee chair or appointing officer.

We're aware that these two approaches can sound overly psychological and intrusive. But note that most executive recruiters are not psychologists and no college needs to psychoanalyze anybody before hiring a registrar. What your committee should ponder here is that there is an important area of knowledge about candidates—their personal makeup and work orientation—that is crucial to performance and that more can be known about.

How a committee might inform itself about these matters will depend on its own sense of missing information, available time, committee expertise, and the position's importance. On the latter score, elaborate interviewing or testing would likely be justified only for certain senior-level positions, most likely those that entail high latitude or discretion and raise a clear need for executive abilities—the hiring of an entrepreneurial head of a new distance-learning operation, for example. For academic positions like a deanship or division chair, there is little warrant in today's search processes for intruding such inquiries; for internal candidates, you might already know much of what these devices would tell you. In any search, you'd be unwise to surprise a candidate by requiring such an interview or test. Any step here should be taken with candidate foreknowledge and with all candidates alike. Any findings should be taken as one piece of evidence only, to be weighed alongside all other evidence.

If you think deeper information about candidates from this domain is needed, our best suggestion is that you talk with an experienced HR professional who can brief you on the ins and outs of this domain, including its legal and ethical requirements. At a later point, where so indicated, that HR person may suggest a professional to do some interviewing for you and a range of possibilities (including assessment centers) on the "testing" front.

stage that they are top-flight and fully qualified (as they are, or they wouldn't be invited), and that the chief remaining question is a fine and mutual one of fit. That approach lends a *positive* air to the visit (and can lessen later disappointment). Contrast this with the interview practices of some campuses, in which candidates are paraded, grilled, and ranked, and which produce "second choices" and "losers" unhappy at the outcome.

Candidate Performance

The best indicator of future performance is recent past performance in relevant tasks, as we've said earlier. The committee has attempted to learn of that performance through extensive telephone inquiries and by direct questioning of the candidate.

A reality, however, is that your information on the matter will always be secondhand, or candidate supplied, and from another setting. Telling as that information can be, it still would be desirable to observe directly the performance of a candidate in a job-related situation in your own setting. What some committees attempt to arrange, then, are circumstances in which the candidate's knowledge, experience, and abilities come to be exercised in public during the visit.

In faculty searches, it's the norm to request final candidates to display their talents in front of peers. A history department may ask each finalist to present and defend a paper; another department may ask candidates to lead a senior colloquium; potential music faculty may be asked to conduct a master class; a candidate athletic coach might plan and conduct a practice.

The analogs for *administrative* search are not always so clear. There is little tradition of performance assessment in administrative search to sanction what your committee might dream up. Certainly you don't want unthinkingly to put the people you're courting on the spot. Whatever you do along these lines must be job-relevant and professionally appropriate.

Given these caveats, the following examples may stimulate your own thinking about the matter.

- Have each candidate present a public, 20-minute talk on a topic of his or her choice relevant to the position, then stand for questions. What depth of knowledge and experience seem

on display? Is the candidate capable of sustained thought and clear speech?

- Have a candidate at the end of a longer, group-interview situation sum up what was covered and learned, what issues were left unresolved, and articulate an agenda for a follow-up meeting. Does the candidate evidence good listening, synthesizing, and planning skills?

- Have a candidate, prepped by an existing background memo, participate in an administrative staff meeting that attempts to resolve an actual situation. What group-functioning and problem-solving abilities are evident?

- Have a candidate deal with an issue critical to the position (e.g., the question of condom machines in residence halls that may face deans of students) in the presence of opposing groups. How does the candidate react to pressure? deal with conflict?

If you decide on a performance exercise, all candidates should participate on the same terms and be briefed about it before they visit. For the sake of consistent, more valid learning, any candidate' performance should be assessed by the same judges (at least three) using job-relevant criteria. What the committee wants is their consensus judgment, in writing.

Candidate–Offer Match

An important individual appointment the committee will schedule is that between the candidate and appointing officer. Allow breakfast and half a morning for it, or an entire evening. Each of the two parties has an important question that needs to be answered during the visit: Can I work with this person?

Candidates will want to ask others in a position to know what it's like to work for this officer; again, this is a reason to schedule appointments with other parties reporting to him or her.

———◆———

As the visit proceeds, the committee wants to do all it can to obtain systematic, usable feedback from all parties with whom each candidate meets. To that end, provide each person meeting with the candidate—individually or in a group—with a form asking just two questions: (a) What strengths did you observe that might contribute to the candidate's effectiveness in the position? and (b) What concerns may have emerged from your meeting with the candidate? Note that you are *not* asking people to rate, compare, approve, or make any summative judgment about candidates; that would be inappropriate, given the limited exposure they had to each. Have, too, a sure plan for collecting these feedback sheets, and supplement it with a provision for electronic feedback. Assign two or three committee members the task of reading feedback sheets and e-mail postings and producing a summary report for the full committee's subsequent meeting.

A reality in search is that as soon as a candidate's name is released to the campus, faculty and staff will launch e-mails and phone calls to friends on that candidate's present or former campuses. The committee should make it clear in announcing a candidate visit that any information a campus party obtains about a candidate should be shared immediately with the chair, who will bring it to the committee along with all other feedback. More than one search process has been subverted by a staff member who dredged up a choice bit of hearsay about a candidate—it may be ten years old and from a disgruntled, unnamed party—and broadcast it by e-mail to the entire campus as proof of the committee's perfidy.

Interviews: In Sum

Let's recapitulate our learning about interviews, adding tips and cautions along the way.

1. There are several types of interviews in a campus visit, not one. Know the power and limits of each, deploy forms of the device that fit your needs, and do not over-rely on any one interview for the judgments you're called upon to make.

2. All interviewers (including committee members) need constant reminders about bias and the dangers of stereotyping. Group interviews followed by discussion can be a plus here; groups tend to self-correct the biases of individual members.

3. The large-group interview is best at eliciting *information* from candidates, including their views on substantive issues. Secondarily it can provide you with a sense of people's reaction to candidates, of a person's acceptability to key constituencies.

4. The most productive interviews will be structured, planned in advance, and executed with discipline. It's hard to impose a formal interview protocol on a large, mixed group, though. But you can improve chances of getting the information you need by a bit of cooperative planning and preassignment of topics.

5. Brief (10-minute) pre-interview discussions between a committee member and interview group can help clarify purposes for best use of the scheduled time. Similarly, a debriefing session (20 minutes) immediately following can ensure that you capture important findings and reactions from the group. Put these in writing.

6. Failure to collect interviewer feedback is the bane of search committees. In addition to the step just mentioned, have *every* interviewer (solo or from a group) complete your two-question reaction sheet. Indeed, distribute these sheets in advance so that people enter the interview with your questions in mind; be sure to collect them afterward.

7. Every interview group needs a chair to keep things on track: to protect time for prearranged questions and their follow-up; to prevent a candidate from rambling on; to nip in the bud special-pleading questions or worn-out lines of interrogation; and to ensure the candidate's comfort and opportunity for questions.

8. During group questioning, if the candidate isn't doing 75 to 80 percent of the talking, something's wrong that a chair needs to right. The first skill of all interviewers is to *listen*.

9. Make sure that interview groups do the job you want, but not your job. That is, they should be collecting information and reactions as input to the committee, *not* voting on candidates. (A sample feedback form may be found at www.thesearchsource.org.)

10. Short, individual appointments eat up time and provide too little feedback to your committee. Restrict them to a very few "must see" people, like the president, and to specific people the candidate would like information from.

11. The first purpose of any shorter, individual interview is to aid the candidate in knowing whether the position is of interest; only secondarily may it help assess a candidate. Recall that until the candidate wants the job, the assessment is irrelevant.

Other Inquiries

While the search committee proceeds to talk by phone with a wider circle of informants about candidates, another track of inquiry should be going forward: the check of credentials. That is, someone, perhaps your HR officer, should verify claimed degrees, jobs, titles, and awards. Do not overlook this step. Résumé faking or fraud turns up in 15 to 25 percent of all cases in the corporate world today and certainly occurs in higher education. We all can cite cases in which a committee skipped this step, then had an appointment blow up in its face when a key discrepancy turned up later. Degree certification may be the most important of these items to check; it's easy to do today, thanks to electronic databases.

Telephone employment checks these days seldom yield substantive information about an ex-employee. Sometimes they can, though, especially when done by an experienced HR officer who knows how to find and prompt the right person on the phone. One thing that officer will want to check is this: what is the employment status of the candidate right now? A certain number of candidates are applicants because they're on their way out from wherever they are now—whatever the reason, you should know it.

Concurrently, have a committee member dig into the publications listed on your candidates' résumés. Do the citations check out? What kinds of publications are they? Especially if they are professionally relevant to the position at stake, what views and quality of thought do they display? Thinking of recent incidents that cost college presidents their jobs, we agree that it would be nice to be able to run a plagiarism check on all of a candidate's publications, but that is not so easy.

For upper-level positions, institutions often insist on a report on the candidate's court record, driving history, and credit status. Commercial firms will perform all three checks for a fee of $100 to $200 per candidate, usually within a week or ten days. You need the person's permission for these checks; the resulting report goes to the chair and candidate only. Speeding tickets or maxed-out credit cards may not disqualify a candidate, but they do call for a conversation.

It is always worth running candidate names through a search engine like Google or Yahoo. See, too, if the candidate is a blogger. Often these steps won't turn up much that is probative, but don't skip them: there could be something there, and you want to know it before someone on campus finds it and tries to embarrass you or a candidate.

Now (or soon) one final inquiry needs to be put in motion: that is, for decanal positions or a provostship, sometimes there is an institutional requirement that the appointee qualify for a faculty appointment, or indeed for tenure. (You may want such an appointment to attract a candidate.) In strict confidence, then, the chair needs to run candidate credentials by the relevant departmental officers and faculty committee, to learn in advance who may qualify at what level for what kind of an appointment. If time allows in the candidate's schedule, have him or her meet with the relevant department chair. Don't leave this step to the end, or the request may be taken as an imposition by the department—and give it *de facto* veto power over a pending appointment.

FAIRNESS AND COMMON SENSE IN INTERVIEWING

Christopher D. Lee, PhD, SPHR

A common myth about interviewing is that in order to be fair search committees must ask each candidate the exact same questions—verbatim. This misconception is rooted in the noble goal of having an objective, impartial search. Here are some exceptions to the myth that treating everyone fairly must mean treating everyone identically.

♦ If a candidate has already answered a question while responding to an earlier question, there is no reason to ask that question again.

♦ In all circumstances, the committee should feel free to ask a candidate to *clarify* an answer, *repeat* a portion of an answer that was unclear, or *expound* upon an answer, and to ask an appropriate *follow-up* question to a response.

♦ Individualized *informational* questions are also appropriate to ascertain facts specific to a candidate, such as "How many years have you served on the board of that professional association?" or "Your résumé shows that you were promoted twice while at Flagship State University; did you keep any of your previous responsibilities when you were promoted?"

♦ Each candidate has a unique background; the only way for a search committee to fully understand that background is to ask specific questions about the individual's experiences.

Committees can achieve their goal of fairness and still treat candidates as individuals. There should be a common slate of questions asked of all candidates so that responses can be compared and contrasted. However, it is also prudent to ask additional questions that speak to the particular background and experiences of each individual candidate.

Failing to ask those particular questions limits the search committee's ability to appreciate each candidate's unique potential. Each candidate should be judged by a common and agreed-upon standard and should be protected from capriciousness, bias, and arbitrariness to ensure that their interests and rights are preserved. Search committees should be sure that individualized questions are not a façade for treating candidates differently because of their race, religion, gender, disability, age, or status in another legally protected class.

Dr. Lee is director of human resources at Bates College.

Last Questions

Near the conclusion of a campus visit, a conversation between the committee chair and candidate usually takes place. In it, the chair ascertains what questions remain in the candidate's mind, whether the candidate is still interested in the position, and what obstacles he or she perceives to acceptance of it. "What would we have to do to make this position attractive to you?" the chair might ask.

This is a moment, too, for the chair or appointing officer to discuss with the candidate any lingering issues, such as a health matter that may impinge on how a position is fulfilled, or a special requirement for taking the position (e.g., help with moving expenses or a school placement), or about job-related restrictions (e.g., the candidate refuses to fly). The chair should also ask about any circumstances that, if they came to light, might cause embarrassment. Some chairs ask the candidate where they see themselves professionally five or ten years from now, and what length of commitment they see themselves making to the institution. (In some cases, by prior agreement, it may be left to the appointing officer to ask these last questions.)

The chair or appointing officer at this point might also ask the candidate (as you may have asked references already), "If I called a dozen or two people at random from your campus or town, what negative information would I hear about you that I don't know now?" This is the infamous TORC question ("threat of reference check"), which can lead a prudent candidate to volunteer additional information, which then is followed up. Indeed, the committee should already have come across "negatives" in its reports about the candidate; it makes sense to raise these with the candidate now and have his or her response.

◆

If you and a candidate find you are highly interested in one another, now is the time to end any earlier restrictions and obtain permission to make unlimited reference calls to the home institution. (In rare instances of a touchy situation, this final step of inquiry may be de-

layed still longer, until the appointing officer chooses to pursue this one candidacy in depth.)

A brief exit interview with the appointing officer may also be in order, especially to cover matters of appointment and compensation beyond the purview of the committee.

Upon departing campus, it is usual for a candidate to feel exhausted and exposed. The next day, a friendly call from the chair can acknowledge the feeling, provide a measure of positive feedback, check for questions, and convey a sense of when the candidate will hear next from the institution.

Summing Up

Once screening is done, the focus of a search changes to knowing and courting candidates. The biggest part of that "knowing" takes place before candidates are brought to campus, via steps of telephone work, Web research, credentials checks, and other inquiries. "Courting" is accomplished via frequent, candid communication with candidates, and by honoring their needs to learn in campus visits.

Committee management of candidate visits is emphasized throughout this chapter. Committees are urged to be clear about a visit's purposes, employ different forms of interview to achieve them, educate interviewers about their role, and arrange carefully for the recording of feedback.

Within a few short days of the last candidate's departure, the committee should at last have in hand the critical information it needs to proceed to its recommendations.

CHAPTER 7

Making the Appointment

At long last the committee is ready to realize the main point of its work: the recommendation of candidates to the appointing officer. That officer in turn will need to weigh, offer, negotiate, and conclude an appointment. All parties then need to bring that appointee into the institution and position in ways that set him or her up for success.

The Recommendation

Once the campus interviews, further reference calls, and background checks are completed, the search committee is ready for a final, longer meeting to develop candidate recommendations for the appointing officer. To keep things moving smartly along, this meeting should occur within three to five days of the last candidate visit.

Prior to that meeting, an important step is for each member to read (and read again) the cumulative records and notes assembled about each candidate. This step is often overlooked. "We've been reading about these people for weeks, we saw them on campus, let's get on with it," someone will say. But past notes grow cold in the memory; the glow from a given interview can overshadow what references have quietly been telling you. Do, therefore, what a professional would do (and what you would do as a scholar): mine those notes, learn them in depth, and think about what they add up to. Your data, conscientiously gathered, contain the rich information you need for judgment.

For what may be its final meeting, the committee should set aside a full afternoon in comfortable quarters, in a private room free from interruption, to ar-

rive at its recommendations. All the information you've gleaned so far on each candidate—application materials, findings from your interviews of them, what you learned from the Web, the initial and most recent reference calls, and the feedback from campus parties during the visit—should be on the table. The chair or a subcommittee, as an aid to discussion, might prepare in advance a list of "talking points" about each candidate, maybe even a first outline of a potential report. Don't stint on time: let each person have his or her full say; adduce what you've learned about each candidate, one at a time, item by item. Voting is seldom in order here—polling may be, early in the discussion—but stay with each case until there's a good sense of the abilities, upside, and risks each candidate seems to present.

———◆———

In earlier years, the work product of this final meeting was often a longer written report on the finalists, which was then formally transmitted to the appointing officer. Today, these reports are seldom written. Beyond the time and difficulty of writing them and fears about later use, they never fully capture the feel and tenor of evidence and of committee regard for candidates. In a written "hand off" from committee to officer, too much information can be lost.

What seems to work best, as trust and custom allow, is for the appointing officer to sit with the committee for the length of this meeting. The officer, indeed, may have telling items to report from his or her lengthy meetings with each candidate. But mostly the officer's role is to listen, query the evidence, and hear in person the doubts, enthusiasms, disagreements, and emerging sense behind the committee's recommendations. In lieu of a formal written report, the committee might work to produce an agreed-upon summary profile of each candidate's apparent strengths, limitations, and qualifications for the position as defined, as well as the committee's overall judgment about him or her as an appointee. The committee also transmits to the officer its full file of information on each candidate.

Where schedules, trust, or local custom prevent the appointing officer's attendance, the chair or a subcommittee of three should meet as soon as possible with the officer to convey the recommendations, perhaps using the committee's summary profile as a text.

To Rank or Not to Rank?

A few institutions insist that search committees recommend candidates in rank order. This is *not* recommended. For one, it too constrains the appointing officer's choice—and it is he or she, not the committee, who is accountable for the appointment and lives with the decision. Another problem with ranking is that it tends to force the evidence and distort a report. The committee spends more time justifying the order of rank than on what each candidate presents as a choice. If you've built a strong pool, *all* of the finalists are "qualified" or "appointable" (this should be the form of the recommendation), but each raises certain trade-offs and would take the job in different directions. The best favor a search committee can do for the appointing officer is to make clear the *range* of candidate abilities and potential directions for the appointment. In a committee process where one candidate has

emerged as a clear standout, or an earlier favorite has faded, the tenor of conversation, not a vote, will make that clear enough to an officer on hand.

The damning thing about ranking candidates is that it invites invidious labeling that never seems to go away. Years later, that marvelous appointee from your search may be doing a splendid job, but in the back of his mind and everybody else's, there's the knowledge that he was the "second choice." This is not the way to launch a successful administrator. The remedy is simple: don't attach numbers to choices.

A university in North Carolina employs an interesting practice relevant here. That is, the search committee provides full commentary to the appointing officer without any ranking of candidates. Under terms of its confidentiality agreement, the committee vows to tell no other party ever about those recommendations. The officer in turn proceeds with review of the report, with candidate contacts, and then to an appointment, and agrees never to tell anyone (including the committee) which candidate he or she contacted first, second, or otherwise; who may have been ruled out; or who may have said "no." The agreement protects the committee and officer alike. The aim is to thwart damaging gossip around campus about who was recommended, whether the committee's advice was followed, or whether the appointee was "our first choice."

The Appointment

The appointing officer's options at this point are to follow the committee recommendations, to investigate further, or to reject the recommendations in favor of a reopened search. If the search has been done thoroughly and well, however, with good communication and agreed-upon standards from the start, an experienced executive will think carefully before straying from the committee's advice. Assuming its members are people of judgment (if not, why were they appointed?), the committee's process should leave an appointing officer in a position to initiate contact with a candidate almost immediately.

Parenthetically, making this point should clarify for

a search committee that the appointing officer is the prime constituent for its work. If you want your recommendations followed, have a credible process and work from the start to ensure the officer of its quality.

Upon receiving the search committee's recommendations, the officer should act upon them without delay. The best candidates will wait only so long to be contacted; indeed, they may be in competing searches, or under pressure to remain where they are, or even be getting counter-offers. As days slip by, their interest and availability wanes. Meanwhile, people on campus begin to presume things: that the committee's recommendations were unsatisfactory or that "It looks like our first choice said no."

Prior to initiating employment talks, the appointing officer may want to tap his or her networks for any additional insight about a candidate (doing so with the person's knowledge). For higher-level appointments, officers have been known to hie themselves off to a candidate's campus to check impressions and talk at greater length with the candidate (again, doing so with her or his permission). An officer may invite a lead candidate and family back to campus for a quieter round of talks, which, if events so indicate, may lead to an offer.

One social change that has become ever more important in searches since the first edition of *The Search Committee Handbook* is the tremendous growth in two-career couples. Some institutions, especially in rural areas, have partner-accommodation networks in place. Institutions in metropolitan areas often volunteer to make phone calls or introductions to assist the finalist's partner to locate a job. In our experience finalists expect some degree of institutional assistance with partner employment. The appointing officer needs to be sensitive to this issue. We have seen searches blow up at the end because a partner could not find appropriate employment, causing the finalist to withdraw.

———◆———

Assuming all signs are positive, a frequent query at this point is what is known as a "Harvard offer." The candidate is asked, "If we were able to negotiate an under-

standing, and if I then made you an offer, would you accept?" The conditional phrasing protects both parties while signaling readiness to negotiate. Moving forward, the appointing officer and candidate need to develop a set of understandings that encompass at least the following:

- Title
- Salary, fringe benefits, and other remuneration
- Start and length of appointment
- Reporting and supervisory responsibilities
- Academic, social, or other expectations
- Criteria for performance evaluation, including conditions of termination

These matters are then reduced to writing and tendered in a letter of appointment. Depending upon circumstances, other matters may be included in that letter: personal or office budgets, provisions for leave, confirmation of a faculty appointment or tenure, office changes prior to the start of duties, moving or other allowances, matters of work conditions or office support, prerogatives as to personnel, and any special commitments made in the recruitment process. In negotiations for upper-level positions, the services of an attorney or financial advisor can often be helpful, especially when creative financial arrangements become necessary.

A few comments about three of these matters:

1. Many candidates will expect to realize at least a 15 to 20 percent gain in salary when they move to a position of heightened responsibility. In making a salary offer, it is best to assume that the candidate knows what the predecessor made and has done homework on comparable salaries. Savvy candidates will be aware also of the cost of living in the area. If your institution is in a high-cost state or region, with expensive real estate or high taxes, candidates will expect the salary offer to reflect this financial reality.

2. The bases for subsequent performance evaluation need to be agreed upon now and put in writing—including when they will be applied,

by whom, looking at what evidence, and with what consequences.

3. No appointment is so urgent that an institution should ever force a candidate to leave another position on short notice (e.g., "Start here the week after next or we'll offer this to someone else"). This is unprofessional, unfair, and seldom productive.

Not infrequently, even when things have progressed to the point of a written offer, the deal is still not sealed. The putative appointee may get a counter-offer from his or her home institution, be near the end of a competing search, encounter a suddenly reluctant family member, or just have cold feet. While the candidate deserves several days to think over an offer, the norm here is to expect an answer within a week—longer than that and your other candidates will have withdrawn. To keep those other candidacies alive, a call from the chair or officer telling them that a decision is forthcoming next week can help.

The point of offer is not a time to forget recruitment. If the committee and officer genuinely want a candidate, let him or her know that. We've seen committees send off a Hallmark card, signed by all, expressing delight and pledging support; personal calls from a president to candidate and partner; attractive institutional T-shirts sent to an entire family; even Packers tickets with a note from Bret Favre sent to a reluctant 14-year-old son. Again, let that candidate know the offer is from a welcoming community ready to offer collegiality and support.

Public Communications

When the appointing officer and candidate have reached an agreement, thoughts turn to an announcement, but before any public word leaks out there are private communications to accomplish. The successful candidate first needs a moment to resign gracefully at home. That done, the search committee should be informed promptly of the offer and acceptance; so must any remaining candidates, with a personal phone call

and then a respectful letter. The latter communication is critical. During our focus groups, one finalist reported learning that he had not gotten a job from the institution's website; another read about it in a newspaper, the story gratuitously including his name. We've heard these stories too often not to issue a friendly reminder. If you treated candidates with respect throughout the search, continue that until the very end by keeping all finalists informed of their status and the outcome of the process.

Others to inform include people within the office of the search, institutional officers, the departing incumbent, and any remaining party of interest. Each should be asked to hold the information in confidence until the formal announcement is made.

The announcement itself, beyond purposes of general publicity, should be calculated internally to a further objective, that of contributing to positive expectancy about the appointment. The appointing officer (or the president) communicates that a fine choice has been made, good fortune brings a talented, new person to campus, he or she looks forward to being here soon and working with us, and so on, as we anticipate the arrival. The point, again, is to prepare the way, not for a savior, but for a good person whom we all want to succeed.

Because people care about how they are described in public, and a mistake or wrong emphasis can be damaging, run that draft announcement or media release by the appointee for approval. Extend all these courtesies to an internal appointee, too, should that be the case.

At this point the formal work of the search committee is all but done. It is a good idea to write each of your original 60 applicants (and any other people who helped you specially) a letter telling them of the outcome, wishing them further professional success, and hoping that your college can merit their continuing regard. The committee chair and office assistant should ensure that all records are forwarded to the appropriate office, usually human resources, for storage. The president and appointing officer should write a letter of gratitude to each member of the committee.

Finally, the chair, with comments from members, should draft a memo to the president with advice to subsequent search committees, noting especially its own false steps or creative inventions not covered in this *Handbook*, and send a copy of that memo to www.thesearchsource.org. Your one- or two-page memo should address what worked especially well, why, and any recommendations for future searches in this area or in similar ones.

Helping the Appointee Succeed

Corporate-personnel literature documents what you'd expect out of common sense: that how an individual enters an organization (the "induction") greatly colors his or her attitudes toward it, and people's attitude toward the newcomer. A person who starts with good briefings, proper introductions, and time to learn enters with positive attitudes all around.

What the literature also says is that most companies are best at orienting lower-level employees. Even in academe, we have people to orient students, administrative assistants, even TAs; but who is in charge of the induction of a new vice president or director of an office? The issue matters. More than one recent administrative appointment has gone up in smoke within the first two months.

In the interim between an appointment and the person's arrival, a number of things can be done to pave the way for a smooth entry, things that the appointing officer or a presidential designate should see to:

- Clean up any remaining "messes" in the office of the position, or in offices reporting thereto. Don't use the fact of a new arrival to delay what should have been done earlier: a "bad apple" fired, a vendor changed, and so on. Consult the appointee, but don't leave him or her a piece of dirty work as the first order of business.

- If the appointee's office needs to be moved, remodeled, refurnished, or reequipped, do it now, before arrival, perhaps with quiet consultation beforehand; never put an incoming person in the position of looking like a big spender or favored case.

- Get your new person into the institutional communications loop: campus newspapers, e-mail distribution lists, and so forth. This is for purposes of informing, avoiding surprises, and building knowledge of institutional culture and how things operate.

- Invest in the newcomer's readiness by funding exploratory visits both to campus and for house hunting as well as attendance at workshops reflecting new responsibilities *and* by not intruding upon vacation time.

- Assign a regular contact person or mentor—maybe the appointing officer, or someone in the president's office—to help the newcomer stay in touch, prepare, and make transition arrangements.

A further idea is to allow time—a week to a month, depending on the position—for the person to arrive and ease into responsibilities. So often a new person comes aboard to be besieged from day one with dozens of small, urgently pressed matters—understandable if the office has been vacant for a while, but intensely frustrating to a newcomer who may not even know yet how the phone system works. What he or she needs is a bit of early-arrival space and time to read files, visit with people, learn the history, get on top of institutional systems and rules, and in general figure out how to operate. A clear signal from the appointing officer to all campus parties is needed to create such an interlude. Of course it also requires that a new dean, for example, arrive midsummer, not two days before the start of fall semester.

———◆———

Once the appointee is on campus, or even before, there is one further, informal role that search-committee members may have an opportunity to play, or at least

WHEN SEARCHES "FAIL"

Even the best conceived and executed search can wind up without an appointment: the finalist group just didn't have the talent you were hoping for; or the committee's choice wasn't that of the appointing officer or of colleagues on campus; or an obviously "best qualified" appointee—the one everyone fell in love with—takes another offer, develops a health problem, or runs into a family complication. Stuff happens.

But as Barbara Taylor of Academic Search cautions, the only search that truly "fails" is the one that leads to a wrong appointment.

When a search hasn't resulted in an appointment, the ball is in the appointing officer's court. A veteran officer knows that the chances of any given search succeeding in an appointment are at best 80 to 90 percent and tries to keep a backup plan active. This may include making an interim appointment, getting an "acting" to continue, assigning duties to other parties, or perhaps making an internal appointment for a set term. None of these arrangements is ideal, but the work of an office must continue.

The trickier question is that of whether and when to continue the search. The starting point here is with what you learned from the first search: As best we can know, why exactly didn't it result in an appointment? Did we set requirements so high that talent was scared away? Was the recruitment as diligent as could be? Did the position's challenges put candidates off? Was the salary competitive? Did the committee and officer have the same sense of what was needed? Were we done in by campus politics? the cost of housing? partner-employment issues? Did other institutions similar to ours searching for the same position meet with success? Did they—should we—use a consultant? You want to get the best answers you can to these questions. The worst scenario would be to repeat the same steps to the same nonresult. Whatever misfired the first time around, now is the time to confront it.

The question of when to restart a search will likely depend on what interim arrangements are possible and on what time of the year it is. If it is February, press on; if it's July and an interim is working out well, it may be best to wait.

Reconstituting a search is also a time to renegotiate terms of continuance of the search committee itself. Not infrequently, committee members will be disappointed, even disheartened; some members won't have the energy or heart for another go-around, while others will feel too vested in the outcome to quit. It may be time, then, for some reshuffling of committee membership, even a new chair.

In one search we observed (it had come up empty-handed just at spring commencement) the committee and appointing officer reversed roles. By agreement, the officer assumed summertime responsibility for recruiting and screening candidates, with the committee in reserve to vet and recommend (or not) candidates the officer thought might be appointable. It worked, and resulted in an appointment on the first of November.

As for restarting a search, there are at least two options. One is to begin over, with fresh people, new advertising and recruitment, and so on, perhaps in the following year, with new determination and earlier errors corrected. A second is simply to continue the existing search by selectively recruiting new candidates one at a time and bringing in for review those who seem most promising (what the North Carolina institution essentially did). Not surprisingly, many continued searches meet with success. On its side, the committee is now in a position to be much clearer about what it is looking for. From a candidate's perspective, the opportunity to avoid being in a large pool and drawn-out process, and to meet directly with the committee at its invitation, is attractive.

offer to the person they helped choose—to be a short-term sounding board or "kitchen cabinet." Often a newcomer will value off-the-record advice from friends vested in his or her success—which problem to tackle first, who are the people to get to know, how to relate to the interim, what are the politics of such and so, how did my remarks go over? Any sessions of this type, of course, would be entirely confidential and at the call of the officeholder.

At a somewhat greater level of formality, and for senior positions especially, some institutions appoint a transition committee to oversee the changing of the guard in an office. Such a group might, for example, arrange appropriate events for the departing office-holder, help with interim arrangements, and host orientation and welcome occasions for the incoming appointee. Often, the chair of the search committee will be part of that group.

From a search committee's standpoint, this final step of proffered help echoes and completes the charge issued in chapter 1: to help the institution find, appoint, and bring aboard a person who will *succeed*.

Looking Ahead

In the introduction, we noted the many changes that had occurred since 1987 and publication of the original *Search Committee Handbook*. More changes are sure to come, at a faster pace still. Things we recommend now may not work on your campus in the future. Legal, governance, and technological changes will supersede today's "best practice."

Happily, American higher education is blessed with inventive minds ever on the watch for better approaches. What you find in these pages is a distillation of the experience and advice of dozens of search veterans, offered up freely—like this *Handbook* itself—at one point in time for the good of the whole. As new ideas emerge, we'll post them on www.thesearchsource.org, and at a later point produce an entirely new version of this publication. If your own search turns up a new idea or better way, share it with us and your colleagues nationally by posting it to www.thesearchsource.org.

Thank you!

Web Sites, Resources, and Associations

Introduction

The Chronicle of Higher Education www.chronicle careers.com

Chapter 1

CUPA-HR (College and University Professional Association for Human Resources) www.cupahr.org

American Council on Education (ACE) www.acenet.edu

Association of American Colleges and Universities (AAC&U) www.aacu.org

League for Innovation in the Community College www.league.org

National Association of College and University Business Officers www.nacubo.org

Chapter 2

For information about sunshine laws go to www.agb.org and by searching for "sunshine," you will find a number of articles, especially one in 2004 by James C. Hearn, Michael K. McLendon, and Leigh Z. Gilchrist entitled "Governing in the Sunshine: Open Meetings, Open Records, and Effective Governance in Higher Education."

Chapter 3

NASPA: Student Affairs Administrators in Higher Education www.naspa.org

American College Personnel Association (ACPA) www.acpa.nche.edu

Chapter 4

The Chronicle of Higher Education www.chronicle careers.com

Black Issues in Higher Education www.blackissues.com

Hispanic Outlook www.hispanicoutlook.com

Community College Week www.ccweek.com

Higher Education Directory information available at www.hepinc.com

American Association for Higher Education (AAHE) www.aahe.org

Association of American Colleges and Universities (AAC&U) www.aacu.org

AAUP (American Association of University Professors) www.aaup.org

ACE Office of Women in Higher Education, Center for Racial and Ethnic Equity, and ACE Fellows www.acenet.edu

AASCU'S Millennium Leadership Initiative Fellows (American Association of State Colleges and Universities) www.aascu.org

Higher Education Resource Service (HERS) Summer Institute for Women in Higher Education Administration www.brynmawr.edu/summerinstitute/hers.html

Harvard Graduate School of Education's Institute for Educational Management and Management Development Program gseweb.harvard.edu/~ppe/highered/index.html

American Association of University Professors (AAUP) www.aaup.org

Additional Notes

An extremely valuable website is the companion to this publication, The Search Source, which can be found at www.thesearchsource.org. There you will find links to all the sites referred to in the *Handbook*.

Another recommendation: CUPA-HR also has a series of publications on interviewing and reference checking.

A website that your HR office may use is the Equal Employment Opportunity Commission site, www.eeoc .gov, which includes documents related to discrimination prohibited in many areas of the search process like hiring and firing, job advertisements, and recruitment.

Annotated Bibliography

If you wish to delve more deeply into this topic, here are some good places to start. There are many articles that address various aspects of the search process; these can easily be found through a search engine such as ERIC. *The Chronicle of Higher Education* Careers section often includes pertinent articles on the search process—usually from the candidate's perspective. These perspectives can be translated into lessons for academic search committees.

An Internet search will also lead you to the many institutional websites with pages of solid recommendations and good advice. You may also find resources available through your discipline; the American Library Association, for example, published *Recruiting the Academic Librarian: A Companion to the Search Committee Handbook* (1991).

The *Search Committee Handbook* has a companion website, www.thesearchsource.org, with articles, links, examples of interview questions and related documents, and much more.

Caitlin Anderson
Research Associate

Albert, S. (2000). *Hiring the chief executive: A practical guide to the search and selection process.* Washington, DC: National Center for Nonprofit Boards.

Published by BoardSource, a national association for nonprofit boards, formerly the National Center for Nonprofit Boards, this booklet addresses timelines and logistics of hiring and includes sections on planning and setting priorities. Most helpful are the appendices with sample letters, interview questions, and rating forms.

Garrison, S. A. (1989). *Institutional search: A practical guide to executive recruitment in nonprofit organizations.* Westport, CT: Praeger Publishers.

While Garrison draws his examples mostly from experience with searches for college presidents, his lessons and recommendations can be translated to any level search. He not only addresses the nature of search committees and the politics involved, but devotes an entire chapter to the critical issue of confidentiality.

Higgins, J. M., & Hollander, P. A. (1987). *A guide to successful searches for college personnel: Policies, procedures, and legal issues.* Asheville, NC: College Administration Publications.

Higgins and Hollander open this text with the recommendation that search committees be provided with training in legal issues surrounding search and employment. While they describe in fairly standard fashion common search steps, each chapter in this book concludes with a section entitled "Legal Concerns." Most helpful are the numerous examples of advertisements, rating sheets, and sample questions for interviews.

Lee, C. D. (2000). *Search committees: A tool kit for human resource professionals, administrators, and committee members.* Washington, DC: College and University Professional Association for Human Resources.

Lee's *Tool Kit* can serve as a training manual, reference manual, or how-to guide depending on one's role in the search process. Tips, checklists, and case studies make this an easy-to-use manual. Of particular interest is Chapter 5 "Interviewing Applicants," which includes ten separate exhibits ranging from a sample interview schedule to a list of "Interview Questions to Avoid." See also *Interview Guide for Supervisors*, 5th ed. (1998) by Mary Ann Wersch, also available from CUPA-HR.

Rosse, J. G., & Levin, R. A. (2003). *Academic administrator's guide to hiring.* San Francisco: Jossey-Bass.

The authors begin with the assertion that we are often prone to "ritual hiring" in academe. They present a structure for hiring based on the principles of 1) performance orientation, 2) systematic information gathering, and 3) rational, realistic decision making. Rosse and Levin suggest that it is critical to link hiring to mission and include an entire chapter on the legal and social context of hiring.

Seldin, P., & Higgerson, M. L. (2002). *The administrative portfolio: A practical guide to improved administrative performance and personnel decisions.* Bolton, MA: Anker Publishing Company

The *Administrative Portfolio* is a logical extension of the now familiar student and teaching portfolios. While suggested as a tool for evaluation of administrators and a tool for improvement of administrative effectiveness, the portfolio also could be used in the job search process—to be requested by a search committee as part of an application package or provided by a candidate to supplement a vita.

Sessa, V. I., & Taylor, J. J. (2000). *Executive selection: Strategies for success.* San Francisco: Jossey-Bass.

The Center for Creative Leadership has studied executive selection for years and has published research results and annotated bibliographies. The Center has identified strategies for pinpointing the right person for the job. While selection in the corporate world differs from the academic setting, there are valuable lessons and suggestions included here.

Turner, C. S.V. (2002). *Diversifying the faculty: A guidebook for search committees.* Washington, DC: Association of American Colleges and Universities.

AAC&U has published a thorough resource aimed at faculty recruiting. The steps outlined and Carolyn Turner's recommendations are appropriate for administrative hiring as well. The monograph begins with a chapter highlighting the importance of mission and institutional analysis. An important section for all search committees to read is "Debunking the Myths" around diversity hiring. In addition to the appendix we have included in this book, Turner includes extensive annotated web and print resources to assist in recruiting diverse candidates.

Acknowledgments

Extensive literature reviews were conducted throughout the preparation of the *Handbook*. As with the first edition, it became apparent that literature reviews needed to be supplemented with the advice and experience of colleagues from across higher education.

We convened seven focus groups around the country on key issues in the search process and found thoughtful colleagues whose comments, suggestions, and stories are reflected on every page of the *Handbook*.

Immeasurable contributions were made by the project's Advisory Board, eleven colleague-friends who set the early course, helped in countless ways through the year, then devoted many dozens of collective hours to our drafts. We also benefited from the advice of five additional colleagues who read every page of the manuscript and whose feedback and criticisms, on small and large issues, has made the *Handbook* stronger and more sensitive to the differences in searches by sector.

The resulting *Handbook* is not, as noted in the Introduction, a committee document; responsibility for its contents rests solely with the authors. Even so, the stories and advice of these people made this *Handbook* what it is.

Participants at Focus Groups

Innovations 2004, San Francisco, California
March 1, 2004
Convened by Jane Lawrence and Caitlin Anderson

Lanier Byrd, Vice President of Academic Affairs, St. Philips College

Hank Dunn, Vice President for Student Services, Sinclair Community College

Richard Fleming, Vice President for Instruction, New Mexico Junior College

Douglas Heesten, Vice President of Institutional Advancement, Cincinnati State Technical and Community College

Ireve Kovala, Vice President of Academic Affairs, Oakton Community College

Maureen Murphy, Vice President for Instruction and Student Development, Wytheville Community College

Dieter Pape, Vice President, Customized Training and Chief Information Officer, St. Cloud Technical College

Karen Wells, Vice President for Learner Services and Chief Academic Officer, Lorain County Community College.

University of Michigan, Ann Arbor, Michigan
March 22, 2004
Convened by Connie Cook and Ted Marchese

Evan Caminker, Dean of the Law School

Gregory Cartee, Professor of Kinesiology

Jeffrey Frumkin, Director, Academic Human Resources

Karen Gibbons, Chief of Staff, Office of the Provost and Executive Vice President for Academic Affairs

James Hilton, Associate Provost

John King, Dean of the School of Information

Patricia M. King, Director, Center for the Study of Higher and Postsecondary Education

Gary Krenz, Special Counsel to the President

Earl Lewis, Dean of the Rackham Graduate School

Lester Monts, Senior Vice Provost and Senior Counselor to the President for the Arts, Diversity, and Undergraduate Affairs

Peter Polverini, Dean of the School of Dentistry

Lisa A. Tedesco, Vice President and Secretary of the University

Laurita Thomas, Associate Vice President and Chief of Human Resources

Anthony Walesby, Senior Director of the Office of Institutional Equity

Janet Weiss, Associate Provost for Academic Affairs

Melissa N. Wiersema, Special Projects Coordinator, School of Social Work

Karen Wolff, Dean of the School of Music

NASPA Annual Conference, Denver, Colorado
March 29, 2004
Convened by Jane Lawrence and Caitlin Anderson

Matt Caires, Assistant Dean of Students, University of Wyoming

Jill E. Carnaghi, Director of Campus Life and Assistant Vice Chancellor for Students, Washington University

Ray Heath, Vice President for Student Life, Marywood University

Valery Oehler, Director of Residence and Student Life, University of California, Merced

Joy Pehlke, Graduate Assistant to the Vice Provost for Undergraduate Education, University of Vermont

Kim Reichert, Assistant to the Vice President for Student Affairs, University of Wyoming

AAHE National Conference Focus Group
April 2, 2004
Convened by Jane Lawrence and Nancy Sansalone
Special thanks to notetaker Beatriz Sapiens, AAHE intern

Donna Bergh, Special Assistant to the Provost, Portland State University

Patricia Senn Breivik, Dean of University Library, San Jose State University

Margaret W. Cohen, Interim Associate Vice Chancellor, Academic Affairs and Director of the Center for Teaching and Learning, University of Missouri-St. Louis

Iain Crawford, Vice President for Academic Affairs, The College of Wooster

Charles Harrington, Assistant Vice President for Academic Affairs, University of Southern Indiana

Kate Harrington, Associate Vice President for Academic Affairs, University of Massachusetts

Fred Maryanski, Senior Vice Provost, University of Connecticut

Jeanne A. Phelps, Assistant Vice President for Academic Affairs, Southwest Missouri State University

AAHE National Conference Roundtable
April 3, 2004
Convened by Jane Lawrence and Nancy Sansalone

Khanh Bui, Associate Professor of Psychology, Pepperdine University

Debra Busacco, Director of Center for Teaching and Learning Excellence, University of Scranton

Michael Collins, Acting Academic Vice President, Memorial University of Newfoundland

George E. Connor, Associate Professor of Political Science

Susanna Maxwell, Vice Provost for Academic Personnel, Northern Arizona University

Marilyn McKenzie, Associate Provost for Educational Programs, George Mason University

JoAnn Moody, Diversity Consultant, San Diego, California

Joseph Morreale, Provost and Executive Vice President for Academic Affairs, Pace University

Kerry Webb, Director of Higher Education, Dallas Baptist University

C.B. Wilson, Associate Provost for Academic Personnel, West Virginia University.

Phoenix, Arizona
April 20, 2004
Convened by Ted Marchese with assistance from Caitlin Anderson

Louis S. Albert, President, Pima Community College, West Campus

Gerardo de los Santos, Vice President and Chief Operating Officer, League for Innovation in the Community College

Naomi O. Story, Faculty Director, Center for Teaching and Learning, Mesa Community College.

Boston, Massachusetts
April 23, 2004
Convened by Margot Lansing, Chris Lee, and
Ted Marchese

Carolyn Everette, Assistant Dean of Human Resources, Harvard School of Public Health

Sandra T. King, Vice President for Marketing, Communication and Public Affairs, Bentley College

Judith McLaughlin, Professor, Harvard School of Education

Cheryl Presley, Vice President for Student Affairs, Boston College

Ronné A. Patrick, Dean of Admissions, Northeastern University

Katherine N. Pendergast, Vice President for Human Resources Management, Northeastern University

Jacqueline Peterson, Vice President for Student Affairs, Holy Cross College

Anita Ulloa, Director of Human Resources, Boston College.

Reviewers of the Second Edition of the *Handbook*
(in addition to the Advisory Board)

Jill E. Carnaghi
Director of Campus Life and Assistant Vice Chancellor for Students
Washington University

Gail F. Latta
Associate Vice Chancellor for Academic Affairs
University of Nebraska, Lincoln

Jeffrey S. Johnson
Assistant to the President
University of Puget Sound

Naomi O. Story
Faculty Director, Center for Teaching and Learning
Mesa Community College

Laura B. Wrubel
Executive Assistant to the President
SUNY-Geneseo

Advisory Board

Louis S. Albert
President
Pima Community College, West Campus

Constance E. Cook
Director, Center for Research on Learning and
    Teaching
Associate Professor of Higher Education
Adjunct Associate Professor of Political Science
University of Michigan

Gerardo E. de los Santos
Vice President, Chief Operating Officer
League for Innovation in the Community College

Judith Dozier Hackman
Associate Dean
Director, Teaching Fellow Program
Yale College

James M. Heffernan
Vice President for Student Affairs and
    Educational Services
SUNY College of Environmental Science & Forestry

Adrianna Kezar
Associate Professor
Rossier School of Education
University of Southern California

Margot Lansing
President
Lansing & Associates

Christopher D. Lee, Ph.D., SPHR
Director of Human Resources
Bates College

Lisa Mets, Ph.D.
Executive Assistant to the President
Eckerd College

Nancy Gaffney Sansalone
Vice President
American Association for Higher Education

Valerie I. Sessa
Assistant Professor of Psychology
Montclair State University

About the Authors

THEODORE J. MARCHESE has been a senior consultant with the Academic Search Consultation Service since 2000. Earlier he served as vice president of the American Association for Higher Education and as executive editor of *Change* magazine. Prior to AAHE, he served 14 years as an administrator and faculty member at Barat College—in the course of which he served on many search committees. His degrees are from Rutgers (B.A., English), Georgetown (J.D.), and Michigan (Ph.D.).

JANE FIORI LAWRENCE is vice chancellor for student affairs at the University of California, Merced. Before UC, she was vice provost for undergraduate education at the University of Vermont and directed the University Honors College at Washington State University and the University Honors Program at the University of Maryland, College Park. In the course of her career, she has served on, chaired, and appointed numerous search committees. She holds degrees in modern European history from Cal Poly, San Luis Obispo (B.A.), San Diego State University (M.A.), and the University of Maryland, College Park (Ph.D.).

About the Research Associate

CAITLIN ANDERSON received a B.A. in sociology and a Ph.D. in higher education and student affairs from Indiana University with a focus on faith development. She was research associate for AAHE's Assessment Forum and special assistant to the president of the University of Vermont, which gave her many opportunities to staff and serve on search committees. In addition to this project, Caitlin is currently working with the Governor's Task Force on Higher Education under the umbrella of the Commission for Higher Education in New Mexico.

About AAHE

AAHE was an independent, membership-based, nonprofit organization dedicated to building human capital for higher education.

About Academic Search Consultation Service

The Academic Search Consultation Service is a nonprofit organization founded in 1976 and based in Washington, D.C. Its mission is to provide knowledgeable, affordable assistance to colleges and universities searching for presidents and senior administrators. Academic Search's roster of senior consultants currently numbers 22; since 2000, it has assisted over 250 campuses. The authors gratefully acknowledge the help of Academic Search consultants in the preparation of this manuscript.

Index